Restorers of the Breach

Fred Garcia

Mobile, Alabama

ISBN 978-1-58169-643-1
For Worldwide Distribution
Printed in the U.S.A.

Axiom Press
P.O. Box 191540 • Mobile, AL 36619
800-367-8203

Contents

Acknowledgments

To my beautiful and loving wife, Michele. You are the reason I know grace, mercy, and restoration so very well. God has demonstrated His unconditional love for me so amazingly through you—thank you for never giving up on me! And in spite of being my first editor, you are STILL my best friend. Thank you so much for your patience and encouragement in this project.

To my wonderful children, Hannah, Elissa, and Joshua. What a privilege to share this adventure with you. You have been some of my biggest inspiration throughout the years, and I greatly appreciate how you have cheered me on every step of the way. What a privilege to be your Dad! I look forward to new adventures together!

To Pastor Tim Davies and Jennifer Widmer. Thank you so much for helping out with the early editing. Your candor and feedback have proven invaluable in the process.

Last, but most certainly not least, to my parents Jake and Elaine. You were the first to inspire me to reach for something more, something higher than just what I saw around me. You have stood beside me in my failures and went out of your way to celebrate my every achievement. I have learned much of my heavenly Daddy's love and generosity throughout the years, but all of it has been built upon the strong foundation which you laid...so it is with great pleasure that I dedicate this book to you!

Preface

When God began speaking to me about writing a book over nine years ago, I thought He was crazy. After all, why would God pick a guy who was unknown and unqualified to write about anything? However, when God speaks, the unqualified becomes qualified, the unbelievable becomes believable, life changes…and so do you.

Each generation is charged with the task of promoting and defending God-ordained liberties and freedoms, yet many still have no clear idea what that means, much less where to begin. Is it a lack of information? No, we are inundated and saturated with information each and every day; in fact, therein lies part of the problem. How do we process and filter that information? How do we discern who and what is reliable? What things need to be acted on? These are great questions! However, obtaining more information is not the answer. While information overload is indeed a barrier that needs to be overcome in our quest to secure and promote freedom, perhaps greater still is the cancerous growth of division among the American people. Therefore, as Americans we need to be reminded once again of the common ground upon which we stand. To be reminded of our commission (our common mission) as those who are called to the work of restoration in order that this nation in which we live may step into the fullness of all that she was created to be. My part is to simply provide some revelation along with various tools which we can use as we continue in the hope of this restoration. Let's look to our nation's former days of glory, as we press on to a future which far surpasses them.

When I began this project almost nine years ago, I worried that this was not a book that looked like anything else out on the market. It didn't look popular or trendy. It still doesn't, and I've slowly come to realize the beauty of that revelation!

Restorers of the Breach was written with the purpose of encouraging, equipping, and the building up the people of America as we focus upon those things that draw us together as freedom-loving Americans. We are indeed standing at a critical point in the history of this great nation. Despite the enormous challenges which we now face, I believe that her best years are yet to come!

I do not doubt that our country will finally come through safe and undivided. But do not misunderstand me...I do not rely on the patriotism of our people...the bravery and devotion of the boys in blue...(or) the loyalty and skill of our generals...But the God of our fathers, Who raised up this country to be the refuge and asylum of the oppressed and down-trodden of all nations, will not let it perish now. I may not see it...I do not expect to see it, but God will bring us through safe. —*Abraham Lincoln*

Part One

Rekindling the Spirit
of Revolution

I did not consider it any part of my charge to invent new ideas, but to place before mankind the common sense of the subject, in terms so plain and firm as to command their assent.

—Thomas Jefferson

~ One ~

THE ESSENCE OF SOLIDARITY

RUNAWAY TRAIN SEAT

Frederick Douglass had a death grip on his seat. At a height of over six feet, and weighing some two hundred pounds, nobody would be removing this unrelenting brick wall of a man from his train seat anytime soon. Nonetheless, Douglass was still faced with one small problem: His seat was no longer connected to the train.[1]

Just prior to this, Douglass had purchased a first-class train ticket. It was typical, and certainly more expected at this time, for Douglass to have purchased a ticket to ride in the "Jim Crow" cars, which were behind the first-class passenger cars and placed there to accommodate black passengers. Nevertheless, Douglass was anything but typical, so he bought his ticket, boarded the train, and took his seat in first class. As one might have guessed, it was not long before Douglass was confronted by the conductor and told that he needed to move. His first-class ticket in hand, Douglass challenged the outraged white conductor to "give [him] one good reason" why he should leave his seat. "Because you're black!" shouted the conductor, who immediately called for several strong men to eject Douglass from the train.

However, try as they might, the railway bouncers soon found that they were unable to remove Douglass from his seat. Instead, they chose to rip the seat right out from the train—with Douglass in it—and escort both Douglass and his seat to the train platform, where they were left to sit and watch as the train departed from the station. In relaying this story to an audience some time later, Douglass said that "They should at least have let me travel halfway; after all, I'm only half a Negro!"[2]

A POLITICAL TOSS

"There is nothing that will make an Englishman shit so quick as the sight of [General] Washington." Abraham Lincoln, like his father, was well known for his ability to captivate an audience; a valuable asset for an aspiring statesman. On this particular occasion young Lincoln was amusing a group of men with a tale about Colonel Ethan Allen, who was famed for his role in the American Revolution. As Lincoln told it, this was Allen's response to his English host who had placed a picture of President Washington above his toilet with the sole purpose of irritating his American guest.

Shortly after leaving his father's home in April 1831, Abraham Lincoln swiftly and quite accidentally established himself in the small frontier town of New Salem, Illinois. His flatboat, laden with goods and on the way to New Orleans, had become lodged on the milldam next to the town that spring. Everyone turned out to watch and marvel at the strength of this young giant and his ingenuity in freeing his flatboat from the milldam without the loss of any cargo. As a result, he would frequently refer to himself as a "piece of floating driftwood" when speaking with the people of New

Salem. He quickly endeared himself to the people of this small frontier town as a man of intellect, ingenuity, and unmatched physical strength. Over the course of his next ten years there, Lincoln would try his hand at nearly every type of work that the frontier had to offer, including carpentry, manning riverboats, clerking a store and mercantile, soldiering and army work, postal work, blacksmithing, and land surveillance. He was a hard worker and kept himself open to trying new things, but like many others, he struggled early on to find his true niche in life.

Compelled by his need for steady employment and seeing an opportunity to once again try something new, Lincoln decided to run for the state legislature. Thus he began his first attempt at a political career in 1832 at the young age of twenty-three. Being six-foot-four and strong as an ox, this young man not only had the intellectual capacity to hold his own against more experienced and better-educated men, he also had the size and confidence to intimidate any potential opponents. As fate would have it, Lincoln had the opportunity to demonstrate this very fact in the midst of his first political speech. Seeing one of his supporters being assaulted in the crowd, Lincoln walked out into the audience, seized the attacker by the "neck and seat of his trousers," and threw the man twelve feet! Nevertheless, in spite of an impressive first campaign that demonstrated the strength of Lincoln's character, intellect, and physical prowess, when the votes were finally counted, he had finished in eighth place out of thirteen who were running for only four open seats on the Illinois General Assembly.[3]

A COMMON BOND

Frederick Douglass was a former slave and a brilliant, self-educated man who would go on to lead the fight against slavery in America, and ultimately become a champion of human rights throughout the world. He was one of the finest orators of his time, publishing several books and proudly proclaiming by the end of his life that he had served as adviser, political ally, and friend to six presidents, including Abraham Lincoln.[4] In speaking of his relationship with Lincoln, Douglass declared that "he was the only white man I ever knew who did not instantly make me aware that I was a black man."[5]

Abraham Lincoln, an equally brilliant man, arose from the humble beginnings of a rural farming community. Like Douglass, he too,was largely self-educated. After finally winning an election to the state legislature in 1834, Lincoln decided to become a lawyer, and he taught himself from books that he had borrowed. He was subsequently admitted to the bar in 1837. He went on to become the sixteenth president of the United States, inheriting the incomprehensible task of leading a bitterly divided nation through unspeakable times, and thus establishing himself as the "Great Emancipator."[6]

Two men of different beginnings, different social statuses, different experiences, and yes, different skin color, yet they were two men eternally linked by a common purpose and a common goal. In essence, you might say they *are* solidarity exemplified.

SOLIDARITY

There is nothing like a good game of kickball. Kickball,

soccer, football, baseball—whatever represents the local game you grew up with—my point is that few things make our differences fade away quicker than a ball. For instance, take the smart kid, the jock, the musical kid, the jokester, the pathologically shy kid, and the tough kid, then put them together on a ballfield and with a little guidance you have a ball game! Every kid is now focused on the game and thoroughly enjoying one another's company. The same is true of most sports fans also. Take the doctor, the farmer, and the factory worker, and put them all in the front row to watch their favorite sports team compete, and before long they're behaving like long-lost relatives! This, too, is a great example of *solidarity*.

Solidarity (true unity) is *the bond formed between individuals, united around a common goal or against a common enemy.* Though often born of adversity, that is not required. Its focus is on the common goal regardless of what individuals may or may not share in common. The goal is readily perceived as genuine and authentic, with little or no convincing required. Solidarity can be found between individuals who are unique in any and all aspects, but they come together to form a unit. The parts of any machine, unique in size, shape, and function, form a unit in much the same way, being brought together for a common purpose. As long as each individual member does its part, you have a finely tuned machine. Yet, when all of the parts of a machine look alike and do the exact same thing, you have dysfunction. Solidarity understands the need for diversity, but it does not legislate it (i.e., make it law). It allows people to find their own place based upon their skills, function, and desire—not their social status, skin color, or government mandates. It *encourages* prosperity of body, soul, and spirit, but it does not see the need to regulate it. (Tell the kids they *must* play ball, what position, how long, and dictate how they have to play, and pretty soon no one will want to play!)

From a historical perspective, Lincoln and Douglass not only exemplified solidarity, but they also helped define it. Along with our Founders, and many others throughout the years, they selflessly demonstrated their devotion to the establishment and protection of freedom by choosing to rise above petty differences and thus submit themselves to the bonds of solidarity. For both Douglass and Lincoln, the common goal was, *in part*, the abolition of slavery and the slave trade throughout all of the States in the Union. However, the *fullness* of what each seemed to have in their hearts to achieve was simply this…*restoration*.

RESTORATION VERSUS RELEASE

For the abolition of slavery and the slave trade to have been their ultimate goal is comparable to saying that the ultimate goal of someone restoring an old classic car is to remove all the rust and broken parts—end of story. Is it an improvement? Yes, but what do you gain? A pile of good parts that belonged to a once-classic car! However, the true heart of restoration seeks to go beyond simply removing that which is broken; it goes further by replacing, repairing, and reassembling each broken part so that the end result is a fully restored and functional classic car. Because many of those parts are replaced with newer parts, better-quality wiring, spark plugs, and tires, the restored classic car will always be of greater value than the original.

For Douglass and Lincoln, restoration was the end goal, which went far beyond their desire to merely see the slaves released. The intent was to see them released and restored, accepted, and acknowledged as equal, fully functioning members of society, thereby adding even greater value to the nation as a whole. Their collective desire was to see that every individual, regardless of age, color, or background, be granted the same rights to achieve the fullest potential for which they had been placed on the earth. If we study our history, we will find this truth to be clearly seen and demonstrated throughout their lives.[7] Both Lincoln and Douglass understood all too well that while slavery had continued until that very point in time, it was neither the intent nor the desire of the vast majority of the Founding Fathers that it remain an institution in the United States. Yet, right or wrong, slavery had been permitted in order to preserve the Union in the hopes that by doing so, the entire nation would eventually see this sinful and immoral practice brought to an end. Far from condemning them, *both* Lincoln and Douglass honored the Founding Fathers by choosing to overlook their imperfections and persevering in the work of restoration, building on the foundation that had been laid nearly a hundred years before.[8] To this end, Lincoln, Douglass, and countless others from this period risked, and in many cases sacrificed, their "lives," their "fortunes," and their "sacred honor" in the deadliest war in American history, in order that *all* might be free to enjoy those same rights and privileges.[9]

FREEDOM'S NEED FOR SOLIDARITY

The restoration of a people, and ultimately a nation, was their end goal. Both Lincoln and Douglass were successful in making great strides in further securing, defending, and even better defining our freedoms. Yet as great as their accomplishments may be, they still did not complete the work.

On the contrary, it has been the privilege and responsibility of each successive generation to continue moving us forward and thereby assisting in the process of restoration. Consider this:

> Freedom is a fragile thing and is never more than one generation away from extinction. It is not ours by inheritance; it must be fought for and defended constantly by each generation, for it comes only once to a people. Those who have known freedom and then lost it have never known it again.[10]

So often we look back at historic moments in time and we sincerely and thankfully rest at ease with the thought that freedom has been heroically and even sacrificially established, once and for all. But in doing so, how often do we give the slightest thought as to whether or not that which has been so courageously established by others is *now* truly secure? In this day and age, it is hard for many Americans to conceive that our freedom could be threatened or ever need defending. In spite of the September 11, 2001, attack (and a few events that have happened since, which we may deem as terrorist attacks but remain politically charged), most of us seem to rest securely in the notion that since it has not been repeated, the nation must therefore be relatively secure, end of story. Yet, while the nation itself *may* be secure, this is not exactly the same thing as our freedoms being secure. The former speaks of our nation remaining free from the control of a foreign power. The latter speaks of our freedom within the country to pursue life, liberty, and happiness unhindered by others, including those who would seek to govern us.

Consequently, some of the greatest threats to our freedom are not found in that which others are doing, or even what they are seeking to do to us; rather, they are found in the very midst of this present generation, in the form of *distraction* and *ignorance*.

DEALING WITH A COMMON ENEMY

Let us go back to the analogy of the group of kids playing ball for a moment. What happens if they begin focusing on their differences as they play? They will get *distracted* and pretty soon all that's left is an empty field. Or better still, what might happen if they begin arguing over the rules to the game? Or what if the star kickball player comes out late and wants to join a team? Same result: an empty field! Why? Because they become *distracted* by their lack of knowledge (ignorance) regarding the rules of the game and the question of where the new player belongs (his identity).

While the enemies of liberty are vast and varied, one of the greatest enemies of American freedom right now is distraction. As Americans, we are so distracted by every so-called problem that our country supposedly faces, that we have lost our ability to exercise wisdom, discernment, and prudence when considering matters that are brought to our attention through the endless source of competing media.

As a people we have allowed our politicians, our entertainers, and our national media to tell us who we are, what's wrong with us, what's right with us, why we should, why we shouldn't, what's good, what's bad, etc. If we allow this to continue, we shall certainly end up a neurotic group of individuals whose sole purpose in life is to mindlessly follow orders from anyone who sets themselves up as our leader. In short, we have permitted others to distract us from our common goals.

As a result of this distraction, we face another great danger to our freedom and liberty in this generation. We as Americans have allowed ourselves to become ignorant. As individual Americans and as a nation, we suffer from the fact that we no longer know who we are and this is largely because we no longer remember where we have come from. And as is so often quoted, "Those who cannot remember the past are condemned to repeat it."[11] It is time for us to grow up and decide who we are and who we will be as a nation, as its stewards, the caretakers of freedom, and the very flames of liberty itself. *If we do not know or decide who we are, and who we were called to be, somebody else will decide for us.* We will eternally become easy targets for those who would seek to control us for their own selfish purposes and schemes.

Who are we designed and created to be as Americans, as patriots, as caretakers of freedom? To answer this effectively, it is time for this generation, young and old alike, to once again rediscover our common ground, our place of solidarity. For if, as Americans, we know what a friend of liberty looks, smells, sounds, and, most importantly, thinks like, we can begin to throw out—or vote out—anything different!

Anytime we possess something of value, like freedom, there will be those who will desire to take it away from us. Over the past two centuries or more, many have picked up and carried the sacred torch of liberty to preserve, defend, and more fully define those same rights and privileges established long ago by our Founders. However, it is vital that we understand that, while praiseworthy, their contributions were meant to serve as an example and not a shield. If freedom is to be preserved, it is now our turn to do so, with a firm reliance upon the hand of Divine Providence.

It may sound like a daunting task, but in reality the approach is no different than keeping our kickball game intact. Solidarity begins with a common purpose (the safeguarding of freedom), then the rules for the game are laid out (our Constitution), and when distraction and ignorance interject, they are dealt with swiftly and effectively (which we shall consider further) so that the game can continue on. Before you know it, you are having a great time with people you never expected that you ever could! To that end, let us begin by once again considering *prudence*—better known to most of us as common sense. It may be a bit of an antiquated word, but like the long-forgotten, hidden treasures found in an old dusty attic, its value is far greater than anyone remembers.

RECOMMENDED READING

William J. Bennett, *America, The Last Best Hope, Volumes I & II*, 2006.

For those who truly feel ignorant of their country's history, or those who simply enjoy history, I highly recommend Bennett's work. It's inspiring, readable, and very well-documented.

Notes

1 *New York Times*, "On This Day: February 21, 1895, Obituary: Death of Frederick Douglass," 2010. Accessed on July 5, 2011. http://www.nytimes.com/learning/general/onthisday/bday/0207.html ; William J. Bennett, *America: The Last Best Hope*, Volume 1 (Nashville: Thomas Nelson, 2006), 280.

2 Bennett, 280; William S. McFeely, *Frederick Douglass* (New York: W. W. Norton, 1991), 93.

3 David Herbert Donald, *Lincoln* (New York: Simon & Schuster, 1995), 39–46.

4 The Historical Society of Talbot County, "Frederick Douglass: Talbot County's Native Son," 2002. Accessed on June 10, 2010. http://www.hstc.org/frederickdouglass.htm.

5 Bennett, 386.

6 The History Place, "A. Lincoln," 1996. Accessed on June 10, 2010. http://www.historyplace.com/lincoln/index.html.

7 Bennett, 284, 300.

8 Ibid.

9 The Declaration of Independence; The United States Civil War Center, June 16, 2001, Al Nofi, compiler, http://web.archive.org/web/20070711050249/http://www.cwc.lsu.edu/other/stats/warcost.htm.

10 Ronald Reagan, Ronald Reagan Presidential Library, January 5, 1967. Accessed June 10, 2010. http://www.reagan.utexas.edu/archives/speeches/gospeech/01051967a.htm.

11 George Santayana, William J. Federer, *America's God and Country* (St. Louis: Amerisearch, 2000).

~ Two ~

PRUDENCE REDISCOVERED

THE STUBBORNNESS OF FACTS

It was just past nine o'clock on the night of March 5, 1770 when shots rang out in colonial Boston; the once-tranquil and snow-covered streets were suddenly brimming with chaos and stained red with the blood of American colonists. British soldiers had fired into a crowd of several hundred protesters gathered in front of the Custom House. As a result, five men were killed and several others were wounded. Incited by the Sons of Liberty, popular opinion portrayed the incident as a "massacre" of innocents. With tensions already high due to the rising occurrence of taxation without representation, and increasing attacks upon the rights of the American colonists by the British Empire, the likelihood of a fair and unbiased trial for the British soldiers accused in the incident was slim. Public outrage called for severe and immediate justice. To most it was just a matter of time before these men were tried, found guilty, and hanged for their "murderous" acts on behalf of the British Crown. An open-and-shut case if ever there was one.[1] No attorney in Boston would even consider taking the case for fear of public opinion.

However, where ordinary men cowered in the fear of

public opinion, one man accepted the defense of the British soldiers, firmly believing that "no man in a free country should be denied the right to counsel and a fair trial," regardless of the public outcry. At the age of thirty-four, despite the risk to his reputation and his family's safety, John Adams chose to accept the task of representing the nine men accused of murder in what would soon become known as the Boston Massacre.[2]

Adams had been practicing law for nearly twelve years and had become increasingly active in both local and national politics. John was the father of three children, and soon-to-be four, as his wife, Abigail, was about six months pregnant. The youngest, Susanna, whom John adored, had just turned one in December. Unfortunately, little Susanna did not survive her second winter and died only a month before the incident in Boston. In spite of his grief and his concern for the safety of his young family, John Adams chose to place his personal feelings aside and set himself upon the task of discovering the truth. After careful consideration of the evidence, including interviews with the soldiers and several eyewitnesses, Adams was convinced that these men had acted in self-defense and were essentially innocent. It was not the popular position, but it was the *only* position he could take after fully considering all the evidence. "Facts are stubborn things," he told the jury, "and whatever may be our wishes, our inclinations, or the dictums of our passions, they cannot alter the state of facts and evidence."[3]

Seven of the nine British soldiers were acquitted, and two were found guilty of the lesser charge of manslaughter.[4] In later years, many would look back on the results of these trials and declare a victory for John Adams, the soldiers, and even for the process itself, which allowed for the evidence or lack thereof to determine the outcome. Yet perhaps the greatest victory to come out of these events was that men chose to act with *prudence*, and they did not allow themselves to be carried away by their passions, their personal biases, or the popular opinion of the day.

INFORMATION ROLLER COASTER

Information that is passed on without testing or questioning can be a very dangerous thing to a potentially innocent person or group. It allows for information to be molded and manipulated into whatever form and for whatever purpose is desired. Yet at the same time, checking out all of the facts that come from our mainstream news media or other sources of information is a seemingly daunting, if not impossible task to consider for most of us. Quite honestly, it's much easier to deal with limited information and simply believe that everything our news sources report on is, in fact, true. Whether it is true or not is often irrelevant for many of us, simply because we are intimidated by the thought of trying to sort through all of the information to find the truth on our own. I mean, after all, their job is to only report the truth, right? Perhaps at one time this could have been an honest expectation of our news media, but unfortunately this is simply not the case anymore. Ratings are primary, and truth is secondary. After all, you can't let something like truth get in the way of a good story, right? And in reality, it is no different than any other profession; some people do their job very well and with integrity, while others do not. The bottom line is that these days, all news is biased one way or another.

Likewise, excessive information, especially untested excessive information, can be just as dangerous and deadly as limited information. Unlike in Adams' day, we live in the Information Age, in which we could conceivably spend the rest of our lives attempting to study all the information available on any one topic and still not exhaust our resources. Consider this...when I was doing a search on voting information, I came up with over seven million websites to check out. "Healthy living" yields nearly thirteen million websites. "Religion" yields over fifty-six million websites. And "football news" yields over sixty-three million websites to check out! Spending just thirty minutes per site, two hours per day, every day of the year (including working through holidays) would take a person nearly 4,800 years to get through seven million websites! Even assuming that many of the websites have repeated information, so that the actual number might be one million instead of seven, that would still take nearly seven hundred years, not to mention keeping up with the latest news stories on television, radio, and in print!

With so much information available, it is easy to see why many of us will simply listen to the nightly news and consider it to be completely factual, rather than *potential* truth or partial fiction, which it really is. And honestly, it *is* much easier to accept their conclusions. As Americans, we have become immobilized by the unprecedented amount of information that is available to us each day. Between the intimidating volume of information and the very thought of carefully sorting through it all, we have become easy targets. Commercial, religious, and political messiahs are ready and waiting each and every day to explain everything and save us by leading us down whatever proverbial road they choose... whatever the end may be. Nevertheless, it is true that there *are* times when we can and even should be led by and submit ourselves to others whom we know and trust. But regrettably, we have become far too accustomed to receiving information and making decisions based upon that information without even verifying its truth...just because it's easier to do so in our time-crunched, drive-thru society.

ENTER PRUDENCE, AKA COMMON SENSE

As Americans, it's time we take a break from simply gathering information and begin to test everything that we know, or think that we know. I am not suggesting it is necessary for you to become an expert in every area where you have questions, but I do believe that we as Americans need to become less gullible. To be *gullible* simply means to be "easily deceived, cheated, or fooled." It is time to begin learning once again how to better apply disciplined reason, wisdom, judgment, and skill in discerning the truth for ourselves. In essence, it is time to rediscover prudence!

> PRUDENCE calls upon our ability to use disciplined reason, wisdom, judgment, and skill in discerning the truth of any matter...and in perfection, it relies most heavily upon the voice of Divine Providence.

To most Americans, *prudence* is better known as good, old-fashioned common sense. And as the old saying goes, it is truly *not common* to all. However, this is largely due to the fact that a very strong aspect of prudence has to do with the passing on of life experiences from one generation to the next, something that is sorely lacking in this day and age. We are taught that we should be self-reliant, and that we can learn all we need to know from our prestigious schools, acad-

18

emies, and institutions of higher learning. Yet, while facts are helpful, prudence is a thing better caught than taught. We need to return to the idea of submitting ourselves to a mentor(s) (parent, pastor, coworker, etc.); no matter what our education or knowledge base might be, there will always be infinitely more that we can learn from those who are more highly trained, are better educated, or have greater experience in areas than we do. (While it should be acknowledged that none of these necessarily make a person more qualified or a good mentor in and of themselves, they do increase the likelihood of a person being a reliable source.) In addition to this, there are several other steps we can take in learning to apply prudence in our lives.

COFFEE, ANYONE?

Great wisdom is gained in simply acknowledging that all information we take in is passed through our own personal filters. In the natural realm, a filter takes great volumes of fluid, materials, or other products, and it sorts out or refines it in order to make it more usable or desirable (for example, a coffee filter). In the same manner, we apply filters to all the information that we take in, in order to make it more usable. The better the filter, the better the end product will be (for example, a better coffee filter makes for less chunky coffee). Also, the more appropriate the filter, the better the end product will be (for example, an actual *coffee* filter will produce better *coffee* than would an air filter). When we begin discovering exactly what our personal filters are and how we utilize them (or when we find and apply better, more appropriate filters), our ability to apply prudence grows exponentially.

So, where do we begin? Let's start by considering some

of the filters in our lives. The simplest way to start is by looking at our passions, or to be more precise, our priorities. What is important to us? It's a question that nobody else can answer or discern for us. We all place differing values on people, things, activities, politics, health, etc. Begin by considering or even making a list (mental or literal—I encourage the latter) of what's important to you.

Passions, Priorities, Things That Are Important to Me

Good health
Spending time with my family
Going to the casino
Growing in my profession/career
Partying and having fun
Relationship with God
Etc…
(Once you make your list, rank them in order of importance to you.)

Next, what is necessary? There are things and people in life that are important to us, and then there are the necessities, some of which may also be part of the list of passions and priorities you just made. For example, my job may or may not be important to me, but it is *necessary* in order to pay the bills and do all of the other things that *are* important to me. What are the necessities you have in life? Take a moment to consider, or make another list.

My Necessities… (in no particular order)

• I must work (where I work may also be a passion/priority)
• Paying bills…taxes, rent or mortgage, utilities, credit cards

- Playing Xbox (or watching TV) for two hours at night
- Supporting my grown son/daughter, who is living with me
- Smoking
- Having health insurance

Finally, what are your core values? In other words, what things do you believe to be constantly true in life, beliefs upon which you base your other decisions? We all have a set of core values whether we have thought about them before or not. For example, one of my core beliefs is that stealing of any sort is wrong. This core belief affects everything I say or do in life where stealing may be an option. From facing the temptation to shoplift, to considering whether or not to re-move office supplies from work for my personal use at home, my decisions are based upon this and other core values. Your core values may include, but are not limited to, the beliefs you hold about human life, sex, God, religion, drugs, your personal character (that is, how you feel you should or shouldn't act), war, politics, etc. What are your core values? (Last list, I promise!)

My Core Values...Examples to Consider

I must treat others the way I want to be treated...
　　or, Look out for number one—me!
God loves me unconditionally...
　　or, belief in God is for the weak.
People of a different race/social status can never be trusted...
　　or, race/social status doesn't matter.
Abortion is an acceptable practice...
　　or, abortion is wrong.
The perfect society is based upon capitalism...
　　or, the perfect society is based upon socialism.

Marriage serves no real purpose…
>   or, marriage is a covenant between a man and woman only.

Now, so what and who cares? I thought we were talking about testing the information we take in, right? We are, and we will. However, to do this you must first have something to test. We could simply take random information and begin the process. But if we are truthful, any random information we take in will always first get tested by our own internal equipment—better known to us as our priorities, necessities, and core values, which are themselves based upon even more information in order to form them in the past.

To better test random information, our first step should be to calibrate the equipment (what we hold as priorities, necessities, and core values), which we are using to test that information. Let's consider it another way: If I think I have gold in my hands, do you think I would choose to test it with equipment that may or may not be working properly? No, if I am wise, I will first make sure that the equipment I am using is working properly so I can accurately test that what I have is, in fact, gold. Therefore, in order to begin applying prudence, I must first start with a willingness to critically examine the very things I frequently use to test all other incoming information. Fair enough? Very good, let's move on.

DISCERNING THE HEART

Now that we have our lists, the next step is to go back through them one more time and ask ourself "why?" Why are these things important to me? Why are these truly necessities in my life? Why are these my core values? Or are these things actually important, necessary, or truly core values at all? For example, if you wrote, "It is important for me to go to church," then ask yourself why. Perhaps you will say, "Because it's what I've always done," or, "Because people expect it of me" or "Because it's what my dad said I should do," or, "Because I like spending time with God," etc. Perhaps you wrote, "It's important for me to vote for candidates from the (fill in the blank) party." Again, ask yourself why. Maybe it's, "Because this is how my parents always voted," or, "Because my friend Ron told me some bad stories about the other parties," or, "I just wanted to spite my parents," or, "Because the values of the (fill in the blank) party most closely line up with my own core values." Why, why, why?

I told you that it would not be easy to test these things. But take your time—process and question things. There are few things more dangerous in life than letting your core values go untested, for certainly everything you will say or do hinges upon them.

Now, we are almost done. But before we finish with this subject of prudence, let me say this: I believe in honoring my parents, my relatives, and my close friends, and I certainly do value their input in my life. I would not be half the man I am today without each of them and without what they have poured into me. However, please make a note of this: it is seldom if ever good advice to believe something or act on something just because someone else—whether it be Mom, Dad, your uncle, your best friend, or anyone else—said, believed, or did it themselves. Let me explain. Most parents, including myself, will do their best to teach their children all that they know to be right and true about life and the world. Much of that advice or information may actually turn out to be quite good. But unless your parents, or the other people who are influencing you, have actually helped you to test and discover the truth of a particular matter (which I advise all parents to do!), how do you truly know *why* it is true? Truth is based upon fact or evidence, not other people's opinions, regardless of how much we may love them or trust them.

If we do not test the things that we hold near and dear to our hearts, we will never know their true value. A painting by Leonardo da Vinci, for example, only has value if it has been tested and found to be one of his original paintings. Anything else is just a cheap substitute. Of course, we may feel a sense of disappointment if we test a painting and find out that it is a fake, but if we truly desire to hold an original da Vinci— something of great value and worth—wouldn't we be better off learning that we have a fake, so that we can then choose to go out and search for an original?

There are many decisions that we make daily that are not necessarily life-altering, and that certainly mean very little to anyone else when it's all said and done. However, there are other decisions that we will make, especially those that affect other people, in which it becomes critical that we make the right choices. If you have made your lists, you now have a better idea of what matters most to you in life and what your core values are. Once you have tested these things, you will be far better equipped to use them in sorting through any additional information that may come your way.

Prudence seeks information from the source whenever possible and is willing to consider information both for and against that which is being tested. If I am seeking the truth on a political matter, then I must go to each party, group, or individual represented to see where they stand. I cannot go to just one of them and ask that individual what all of the others believe for their answer will always be biased! In the same way, if I want to know about God, I certainly should not base my opinion of Him entirely on the statements of someone who doesn't know Him or believe He exists. That would be like going to the tabloids to find answers to personal questions about Peyton Manning or LeBron James. The tabloids do not know them, therefore their information will always be biased—and extremely limited at best!

There is absolutely nothing wrong with asking others for their opinion, however to make any sort of educated decision about the more important things in life we need to consider both sides from an unbiased source whenever possible.

So, do we have to test our filters? No. But we should realize that regardless of our choice, whether or not to carefully test and weigh our priorities, our beliefs, or our core values, there will always be consequences to reap in the end for better or for worse. Life is full of choices that mold and shape us into the people we become. We are not victims and nobody makes us. We choose and we are a product of those choices. Likewise, great men and women (heroes) are seldom, if ever, born that way. They are the product of their choices. We'll consider this further in the next chapter.

THE RESULTS OF PRUDENCE

From patriot to president, John Adams was a man like few others in the history of this great nation. Even after years of service to God and country, John Adams still looked back upon his legal defense of the men accused in the Boston Massacre as "one of the best pieces of service I ever rendered to my country."[5] John Adams believed in the cause of independence. It is possible that, had he not chosen to defend these men, the winds of passion would have fueled the cry for independence all the quicker. However, I firmly believe that Mr. Adams knew all too well that if the colonies were to succeed in birthing a new nation, *prudence* and *integrity* were essential foundations for them to build upon and the keys to defining where this nation would stand in an ever-changing world.

The same type of filters we use in better understanding *who* we are and *what* we believe can also be applied to our nation as a whole. Before we can even begin to consider that, however, we must first consider the smallest component of any nation—the individual. We cannot begin to find our common ground as a nation until we know where we stand as individuals. Our priorities, our belief systems, and our core values must be examined, weighed, and tested. In essence, prudence must be applied in learning who we are. In doing so, I firmly believe that we will find ourselves much closer to people whom we once considered fools or enemies than we might have ever believed possible.

RECOMMENDED READING

1. David McCullough, *John Adams*, 2001.

—The television miniseries was good, but nothing compares to the book! *John Adams* reads like a good story, and few authors are able to present solid, factual history in as lively or entertaining a manner as McCullough.

2. Harold R. Eberle, *Christianity Unshackled: Are You a Truth Seeker?* 2009.

—An excellent book for the reader who needs to search

things out a bit deeper, but who desires a resource that's easy to read, historically accurate, and yet holds nothing back. I highly recommend this book for any reader, Christian and non-Christian alike.

Notes

1 David McCullough, *John Adams* (New York: Simon and Schuster, 2001), 65–68.

2 Ibid.

3 Ibid.

4 Ibid.

5 Ibid.

~ Three ~

DESPERATELY NEEDED:
A GENERATION OF HEROES!

In June of 1938, Superman burst onto the scene with Action Comics as one of the first superheroes who could not only leap tall buildings in a single bound, but was also among the first to carry a storyline that would endure for generations to come.[1] Who was the first superhero ever? Well, that would largely depend upon a person's perspective as every generation has had individuals who have risen above what ordinary men or women could do, whether real or fiction, spanning back to the beginning of time.

Whether it is a story about an everyday "Joe" or someone with superhuman powers who fights for truth, justice, and the American way—I love superhero storylines! While I have never become obsessed with any one of them in particular, I do have certain favorites—some for the incredible strength of character they possess, others for their acts of bravery and self-sacrifice, and still others for the wisdom imparted throughout their particular stories. Regardless of the vast and various reasons we have for liking a particular hero, we find some common threads throughout most of their stories. As we continue to search out who we are as individuals and as a nation, it would be helpful to take some time and consider what it truly means to be a hero.

BROTHERS OF ADVERSITY

Marvel Comics has given the world some fantastic, outstanding, and otherwise incredible superheroes throughout the years, including Spider-Man, the Fantastic Four, Captain America, and G.I. Joe, to name but a few. But their creation of the mutant X-Men was absolutely extraordinary—and pivotal. By far one of the most controversial and compelling storylines of its nature, X-Men brought the question of what makes one a superhero or a supervillain to a razor-sharp edge. The creators of X-Men wasted no time in blurring the distinction between hero and villain by inserting themes such as racial prejudice, revenge, and "fitting in" to be pondered, grappled with, and heavily debated, challenging both its characters and its readers.

Basically, X-Men chronicles the struggle between one group of both mutant and normal people, each of which fears and desires the destruction of the other...and another group of both mutant and normal people who collectively desire to settle their differences peacefully and even learn from each other. Two of the most notable characters in this series are Erik Lehnsherr, or "Magneto," who ultimately chose to become the leader of the bad guys, and Professor Charles Xavier, or "Professor X," whose powers and desire to do the right thing positioned him to become the leader of the good guys. Two characters, both of whom experienced pain, suffering, and disappointment in life, but each of whom ultimately chose entirely different paths. While the creators at Marvel certainly draw their own conclusions as to what forces influence and mold their characters, it does beg this question for us to ponder: do we really have a choice, or are we simply a complicated product of genetics, instincts, experience, and environment?

THE ABILITY TO CHOOSE

For years, many have hidden behind the broad claims made by some geneticists that our health and our behavior are predetermined in essence by our genetic code. However, recent research in the fields of behavioral genetics and epigenetics (the study of inheritable changes in gene function that do not involve changes in DNA sequence)[2] is beginning to cast greater doubt on such claims, and even prove otherwise. Recent studies of twins have shown how the same exact genetic code still allows for unique expression in each twin, largely due to things such as what they eat, what they drink, whether they smoke, etc.—things that are directly affected by choice.[3] We might have genes that predispose us to certain physical and behavioral characteristics, but they do not absolutely determine what our choices will be; they do not determine our fate, like a movie script. Think of it like this: Genes are simply the building materials given to each individual. They do not predict a person's success or failure any more than a pile of bricks determines what will be built out of them. However, what a person chooses to do with the pile of bricks he or she has been given—to build a home for themselves, to build a jail for themselves, or simply to lie down on top of those bricks and die—determines a person's fate.[4]

So then, do circumstances, environment, and genetics influence us in any way? Yes, of course—and powerfully too!

Our ability to choose does not magically dispel their influence upon us. However, my point is this: If I acknowledge that I can be influenced by a great number of things, including other people, and yet at the same time I also acknowledge that I do, in fact, possess the free will to make my own choices, regardless of those influences, then in the end I must admit that I am always responsible for my own actions and choices.

HERO VERSUS VICTIM

Choice is the primary difference between a *hero* and a *victim*. From those with superhuman powers to the average man, woman, or child on the street, regardless of circumstances, a person's choices are what make them a hero or a victim. According to *Webster's Dictionary*, a *victim* is simply a person "that is acted on, and usually adversely affected, by a force or agent."[5] In the broadest sense of this definition, both of the characters I described earlier are victims. And, in fact, we are all victims to some degree in the sense that we have all experienced people, things, or circumstances that have adversely affected us at certain times in our lives. However, did Magneto or Professor X—or any of us for that matter—choose to become a victim? No, certainly not. Things beyond our choices and control *do* happen to us. So then, in what context do I say that people make the choice to be heroes or victims? It's all in the response! Look at the following chart to see differences between the two:

VICTIMS	HEROES
Choose to allow the fear that has affected them to influence their choices.	Choose not to let fear be the driving force behind their decisions.
Often choose vengeance or retribution when they are wronged, over restoration or doing what is right.	Choose to hold others accountable for their actions but not at the expense of harming others unnecessarily or doing what is wrong.
See only the interests of self.	See and consider the interests of both self and others.
Seek out all they "feel" that society owes them.	Seek out the various ways in which they can serve society even often at great cost to self.
Choose unforgiveness and experience bondage.	Choose to forgive* and find true freedom! We can still hold people accountable for their actions! More on this in chapter 6.
Are often double-minded or hypocritical, and thus not very dependable; can be seen as unstable. (For example, they may say they hate it when people steal from them, but it's okay for them to steal small things from others, especially if their victim is rich!)	May become misguided and make mistakes, but readily admit their failures and shortcomings and strive to be consistent in all that they do.

Very few people in this life will ever set out from the beginning to become a villain, embracing injustice, lies, and the destruction of dreams. Yet more often than not, those who ultimately become villains first choose to embrace the mentality of being a victim. You see, how we choose to respond to people, adversities, or negative circumstances is what makes us more of a hero or a victim.

Even better, let's consider this in yet another context: the slave versus the freed man. The Israelites of the Old Testament had been slaves to the Egyptians for four hundred years before God raised up Moses as their deliverer.[6] After four hundred years of being slaves, suddenly they were free! Yet being free from slavery in the physical sense did not automatically mean they were free from the way of thinking that was associated with slavery, or the slavery mind-set.

SLAVE	FREEDMAN
A slave typically does the minimum required amount of work to survive, with no motivation to do more.	A freedman typically works each day to get the maximum work done so that they and their household will prosper.
A slave is used to being fed.	A freedman feeds himself.
A slave is controlled by fear.	A freedman chooses to press on even in the very face of fear, for this is true courage!
A slave would rather return to bondage than face an uncertain future.	A freedman looks at the potential of an uncertain future, makes plans, and allows Divine Providence to order his steps.

Note: The use of the term slave in the above table simply denotes a person who holds on to a slavery mind-set.

It took the Israelites forty years and cost them the lives of an entire generation, with the exception of Joshua and Caleb, before they could free themselves from the slavery mind-set and enter into the Promised Land. What has it cost us so far? The degree to which we choose to embrace the slavery or victim mentality is the degree to which we become the hero or the villain in our own story, and thus whether we ultimately prosper or become our own worst enemy.

It would appear that many of us in America (regardless of race) still live (at least in part, if not entirely) in a victim or slavery mind-set. And many of us look for a change in circumstances, such as an increase in our financial resources, as the key, or the ultimate solution to finally fixing things. However, consider this: The Israelites had been set free from slavery; they were given the wealth of the Egyptians; they had God fighting on their behalf to destroy their enemies; God had miraculously delivered them through the Red Sea; and God had even provided miraculous food from heaven, water from rocks, and numerous other signs and wonders. They should have been a pretty happy group of people, right? They *should* have, but they weren't! As a result, all but two of them (out of an entire generation of people!) died in the desert because they wouldn't stop grumbling and complaining, thus demonstrating their lack of trust in God even after all He had done for them. Why? Because they wouldn't let go of the slavery mind-set!

The same thing can be seen today with lottery winners. Many people think that winning the lottery would solve all their problems, yet statistics show that the level of happiness of a lottery winner is at about the same level a year after their winning as it was before they ever won anything.[7] In other words, if we are miserable or happy before we win the lottery, chances are we'll be just as miserable or happy a year later. Why? Because a change in financial status and/or external circumstances does not change our mind-set or the way we think—we do!

As Americans, regardless of our financial status, our ethnic background, our social status, or anything else we have going for or against us, we all share this in common: We have been given the right to life, liberty, and the pursuit of happiness. We have been granted the freedom to make a way in life for ourselves, to choose what we will become or what we will pursue. We have been granted the freedom to choose how we will attempt to succeed in life. We have nearly unlimited resources at our fingertips if we choose to seek them out and utilize them. We live in the greatest country in the history of the planet, and yet all that many of us can see is "doom, despair, and agony"! Oh, I'll admit that bad things are out there, but my challenge to you is this: You are an American—what are you going to do about it? Are you willing to let your circumstances define you and ultimately create your success or failure for you? Or will you listen to the voice of the hero inside yourself and choose to rise above it all?

A true hero refuses to be defined by his outward circumstances, takes responsibility for his own actions, forgives without measure, and is intimate with the concepts of service and selflessness.

Honestly, it is much easier to play the victim than to become the hero. Being the hero requires hard work. Yet the choice and ability to be the hero is within the grasp of every single American. Whatever you choose, just realize that the freedoms that you now have access to have been purchased and defended with the price of blood, selflessly given time and time again by generations of American soldiers and patriots, both men and women, from the inception of this country. Let us honor those who have paid the price for our freedoms by seeking to cast off the slavery mind-set and the victim mentality. Let us continue, or perhaps begin for the first time, to step into all that we have been called to do and to be. It is time for a new generation of true heroes in this nation to arise!

RECOMMENDED READING

1. *HEROES Among US*, Jim Ryun & Sons, 2002.

—Light reading for inspiration. Great book filled with enough heroic motivation for you and the whole family!

2. Max Lucado, *It's Not About Me*, 2004.

—Easy reading, but geared more toward those who are ready to get down to business.

If you are in need of personal assistance in this process, I would direct you to the appendix in the back of this book.

Notes

1 Wikipedia contributors. Action Comics. Wikipedia, The Free Encyclopedia. September 22, 2016, 02:41 UTC. Available at: https://en.wikipedia.org/w/index.php?title=Action_Comics&oldid=740601064. Accessed October 2, 2016.

2 *Merriam-Webster*, "epigenetics," 2012. Accessed on January 28, 2012. http://www.merriam-webster.com/dictionary/epigenetics.

3 Randy Jirtle, *Nova: Science Now*. July 2007. Accessed on June 12, 2010. http://www.merriam-webster.com/dictionary/epigenetics.

4 Jirtle, 2007.

5 *Merriam-Webster*, "victim," 2010. Accessed on June 13, 2010. http://www.merriam-webster.com/dictionary/victim.

6 Exodus 1:1–40 NASB

7 "Prosperity from the Inside Out," 2002–2009. Accessed October 10, 2010. http://www.choosingprosperity.com/lottery.htm.

~ Four ~

REESTABLISHING TRUST

There is no doubt that *all* of the men and women who serve in our country's armed forces deserve our continual thanks and respect. Their steadfast vigilance is vital in securing the freedoms that we enjoy each and every day in this nation. However, among them are individuals with a very distinct honor and heritage, whose valor and devotion often go unnoticed and unappreciated. These are the men and women of our *color guard*. To most, they are nothing more than a group of soldiers who reverently bear our nation's flag, along with other military banners, for a multitude of events, ranging from parades on the Fourth of July, to sporting events, funerals, and military graduations, just to name but a few. While this may be true, there is *much more* to be told of their legacy.

THE COLOR GUARD

Throughout our nation's history, the American flag and its accompanying military flags and banners have been symbols of our solidarity, our strength, and the precious freedoms that we possess. They have been held in high esteem throughout the years by soldier and patriot alike. Yet perhaps they have never been carried more valiantly than by the color guard of the Union and Confederate forces during our nation's Civil War. To these brave men, the flags that they bore were the most sacred items they collectively possessed. As was true in the Revolutionary War, the men serving in the color guard during the Civil War were those who would actually lead a given group of soldiers onto the battlefield. They would bear either the Union or Confederate flag, along with a unit or regimental flag that served to identify the unit to which the soldiers belonged, allowing them to stay together more easily.[1]

It was the most trusted and honorable position for a soldier to be a part of their unit's color guard. Only the bravest soldiers volunteered for this duty, as bearing the flags meant that they would not be able to carry or use any firearms. Once the battle began, the color guard played a key role in determining the outcome, as these soldiers were the only means of effective communication through the loud noise and dense smoke that would settle in as a result of heavy cannon and musket fire. Where the colors went, the soldiers would follow. If the colors stopped, so too would the soldiers; and when a large group of soldiers stopped on an open battlefield, they were sure to become a much easier target for the enemy. Knowing this, soldiers on both sides knew that if they could stop the flags, they could temporarily stop an advancing army unit and thus have stationary targets at which to shoot. Therefore, with the full knowledge that they personally would become the primary targets of the enemy's sharpshooters and infantrymen, the brave men of the color guard would nevertheless march onto the field of battle, unarmed but ready to protect their flags with their very last breath. It was a duty that these courageous soldiers took quite seriously, realizing that their unit was depending upon them to inspire and direct throughout the battle. As they fiercely protected these most sacred items—the flags—they realized full well that it could mean the sacrifice of their very lives once the battle began.[2]

There are few better examples of trustworthiness than those who choose to place themselves in harm's way in order to defend others. Many a veteran of war has said that "there are no atheists in foxholes." But it could also be said that there are no trust issues in the trenches. When you are on the field of battle and depending on the guy next to you to help preserve your very life, any differences you once had between the two of you melt away as you prove your true character by your actions. Trust rises above what makes us different, as we choose to make ourselves vulnerable to one another. It's a choice made by an individual, to look beyond their past hurts, disagreements, social background, or skin color in order to give another individual aid in working toward a common goal. As the flagbearers demonstrated through their choice to depend on their fellow soldiers to protect and defend them, trust always involves risk.

ONE SOLDIER'S STORY

Abridged diary entries of Sergeant-Major C. A. Fleetwood, from Thursday, September 29, 1864:

> Stirred up [the Regiments]...knapsacks packed away...coffee boiled and [the] line formed. Moved out... [We] Charged with the 6th at daylight and got used up. Saved colors....[3]

As part of the 4th Regiment US Infantry, Union Army, Sergeant-Major C. A. Fleetwood participated in the Battle of New Market Heights, near Richmond, Virginia, on September 29, 1864.[4] During their charge on the enemy's fortifications, Fleetwood's regiment moved forward under heavy fire from the well-entrenched Confederate infantry. Continuing the charge in the face of heavy casualties, fellow soldier Sergeant A. B. Hilton, who himself had taken up the two flags from other members of the color guard that had fallen, called out to Sergeant-Major Fleetwood and Private C. Veale. "Boys!" he shouted. "Save the colors!"

Before they could hit the ground, Veale took up the blue Regimental flag and Fleetwood the American flag. Fleetwood continued forward under heavy enemy fire until it became clear that his unit would not be able to penetrate the enemy's defenses. Retreating back to the reserve line, Fleetwood used the flag to rally a small group of men to continue the fight. Afterward, Fleetwood stated:

> I have never been able to understand how Veale and I lived under such a hail of bullets…. We did not get a scratch. A bullet passed between my legs, cutting my bootleg, trousers, and even my stocking, without breaking the skin.

Though it was bravely fought, the battle was lost with heavy casualties; nearly two hundred men from Fleetwood's own regiment of three hundred were injured or killed ("got used up"), including eleven of the twelve men in the regiment's color guard.[5]

For their part in seizing the colors when all others had fallen and for nobly bearing them through the fight, Sergeant-

Major Fleetwood, Sergeant Hilton, and Private Veale were each awarded the Congressional Medal of Honor, the highest award for valor in action against an enemy force. Less than 3,500 soldiers have been awarded the Congressional Medal of Honor even to this day, out of the millions of those who have served throughout the history of this great country.[6] As a further honor, every officer of the 4th Regiment sent a petition for Sergeant-Major Fleetwood to be commissioned as an officer. The request, however, was denied by then–Secretary of War Edwin Stanton, more than likely due to the fact that Sergeant-Major Fleetwood, Sergeant Hilton, and Private Veale were all black men.[7]

When the war began, Fleetwood was not allowed to fight because of his skin color. Many blacks desired to enlist, but President Lincoln was reluctant to let them do so for various political reasons. However, without the consent of anyone in Washington, General David Hunter took it upon himself to assemble and equip the first black regiment in South Carolina in the spring of 1862.[8] As a result of this bold and creative nudging, President Lincoln relented, releasing the good general to engage his enemies "as best he might," thus allowing blacks to begin enlisting, with many of them answering the call to serve their country as the impassioned Frederick Douglass was encouraging them to do.[9]

Faced with prejudice, Fleetwood chose to overcome. Denied promotion, likely due to his skin color, he still chose to continue fighting alongside men of every ethnic background—black, white, and every shade in between. Christian Abraham Fleetwood even went so far as to write the following in his diary at the end of that year:

Saturday, December 31, 1864:
Stormy and snowing all day. So endeth the year 1864.
During which the Goodness of God in preserving my
life and health, has been brought more clearly than in
any other year to my senses. With [a] humbly grateful
heart, for his past protection. Trustingly I enter upon
the New Year.[10]

How does a man faced with prejudice and the injustice of
slavery, which was still rampant within the country he was
defending, maintain a perspective that allows him to overcome?

TRUST AND PREJUDICE

Prejudice in all of its various forms has existed as a primary source of mistrust and disunity among mankind for centuries. Despite our best efforts, we cannot and will not
change the fact of its existence, any more than we are capable
of eradicating death and disease this side of heaven. Like
death and disease, however, the effects of prejudice can be
contained and minimized when prejudice is properly handled
and understood. And like disease, prejudice does not discrim-
inate; it can infect anyone regardless of social status, affilia-
tion, or ethnic background.

Think about it. When a contagious disease strikes, it starts
with the individual; if not contained, it can go on to infect
everyone it comes into contact with, and then eventually
every person that the newly infected person comes into contact with, and so on. Prejudice, like disease, starts with the individual, not the group. (Just let that sink in for a moment...)
When we choose to go beyond simply holding the individual

responsible for their prejudicial comments or actions and begin taking offense at the entire group they represent (or *claim* to represent), we will soon find that, in spite of our best intentions, we have allowed ourselves to be sucked into the disease. So, let's take a closer look at the commonalities between disease and prejudice for a moment.

Because disease is often hidden, we do not always know when we have been exposed to an infected person. So what do we do? First, we learn to recognize the signs and symptoms of the disease so we know what to watch out for. Then, whenever possible, we inoculate ourselves from the disease, which then allows us to come into contact with those who do have the disease but without fear of transmission. Finally, as much as it is up to us, we seek to get help for the individual affected by the disease, so that they can be isolated and kept from infecting others while they receive the treatment they need, whenever possible, to be healed.

When we suspect disease, do we immediately begin treatment? No: Once the signs and symptoms of the disease have been recognized, a person is then tested in some way to confirm that the disease is truly present. The same rule applies when we suspect prejudice. Prejudice is simply making an unfavorable judgment or forming an adverse opinion about someone or something without having the factual knowledge to support it. In short, prejudice is openly playing a fool. The signs and symptoms of prejudice are, therefore, easy to recognize: Simply look for the facts of any given situation, then look for the fool who is declaring the exact opposite of what the facts are telling you. They may come across as hostile, elite, or even very charismatic and convincing; but facts are facts, and those advocating prejudice will always line themselves up in direct opposition to the truth of any subject matter, and they ultimately play the fool whether they realize it or not. Again, recognizing prejudice is actually quite easy—if you take the time to check the facts! So, step one in recognizing the signs and symptoms of prejudice: *Check the facts.*

Step two involves confirming our suspicions. Remember, one of the main tenets of our American judicial system states that we are innocent until proven guilty. Most of us say and do things all the time out of a position of being thoughtless, more so than being purposefully prejudiced or hurtful. For this reason, the vast majority of us in this nation need once again to reconsider or learn the art of clarification. We need to confront the individual whom we suspect of prejudice and give them a chance to clarify whether or not what we heard or saw was, in fact, what they intended. After all, we have all had occasion when others have misunderstood our intent or meaning. No one is infallible in this area. Communication (or lack thereof) is at the center of a fair majority of fights and disagreements. We all get nervous, we all may be tongue-tied, or we might lack the words we need to express ourselves at times. This being true, we need to start by giving others the benefit of the doubt and then tell them what we thought we heard, and give them a chance to clarify. We can say, for example, "Here is what I think you said... Is that correct?" Experience has shown me time and again that most offenses I have picked up against people over the years were merely a matter of misunderstanding, more so than an intentional offense. Therefore, step two in recognizing the signs and symptoms of prejudice: *Clarify.* It is only by taking a *risk* and giving others the benefit of the doubt, and a chance to clarify, that we can begin the process of inoculation.

SOWING THE CURE

Inoculation is simply introducing a disease to the body so that it can begin to produce its opposite, rendering it harmless and ineffective. When we choose to work in the opposite spirit of prejudice, we render it ineffective. First, we must choose to believe the best about others without being gullible, which is challenging in itself. When we begin engaging in relationship with people, we need to give them a chance to be trustworthy, but we do not necessarily need to begin by handing them our wallets. It means that we take a measure of risk (in small steps) and choose to trust them until they prove themselves unworthy of our trust.

Second, we choose to love people with our actions. When we act with love and consideration toward someone else, we will soon find that our feelings begin to change toward them. Love does not necessitate "gushy" feelings for people—feelings will follow actions. When we begin to realize this, it makes loving our neighbors (even the goofy ones) much easier and much more tolerable.

Finally, we must choose to walk in forgiveness for both past and present wrongs. Forgiveness does not necessarily mean releasing a person from being accountable for their actions. It is simply this: releasing yourself from being the judge and jury over another's heart so that God can be. It is only in exercising measured trust that we can avoid the bait of prejudice, and in turn, establish trust with a person or group with which this once seemed impossible. If we want to harvest apples, we plant an apple seed; if we want to harvest trust, we must choose to sow a seed of trust.

Christian Abraham Fleetwood believed in the ideal that truly all men were created equal. He fought for the unity of

46

his country while moving forward with eyes of faith. Faith believes in that which is not as though it is, and it acts based upon that which is unseen. He chose to trust in the relationships that he had established with people, believing that with men like them at his side (of every ethnic background), eventually both slavery and prejudice would be overcome. Yes, slavery and prejudice still existed, but *he* chose to rise above them and recognize them for what they were—*the sins of the individuals, not the sins of an entire race*. He carried the flag in the face of certain death for the freedom of all, even if some of them were not deserving of his sacrifice. Fleetwood's role as flagbearer was one of valor and devotion, leading the way in the midst of the battle; in life he was no less exemplary.

> TRUST necessitates relationship, and it is the firm reliance upon another's character, strength, and ability—devastating when broken and difficult to regain…but not impossible.

Trust, like prejudice, operates at the level of the individual and not the group. It is to be given to those who have earned it. It requires that a measure be given initially to help determine another's character or to allow them the opportunity to *begin* developing character. It is not to be given or rejected based upon skin color, social status, or for any other petty reason. Trust is established as we choose to sow it into relationships. When we are willing to take a small risk and deal with people on an individual basis, we may suddenly find we have many more people whom we may be able to trust, work with, and even enjoy!

RECOMMENDED READING

Christian A. Fleetwood, *The Negro as a Soldier*; 1895.

—As with most heroes of historic origin, their contributions to society often go far beyond what most remember. Fleetwood is no different in this respect. By following the link listed in the bibliography, you will find Fleetwood's work as presented to Congress, honoring the contributions made by black soldiers throughout our military history to that point in time. A short, but very worthwhile read!

Notes

1 Scott K. Williams, "Missouri Civil War Museum," 2010. Accessed on June 13, 2010. http://www.mcwm.org/history_flags.html.

2 Ibid.

3 Christian A. Fleetwood, "Diary of Sergeant Major Christian A. Fleetwood, U.S. Colored Infantry, Fourth Regiment Company G, 1864," 2007. Accessed on June 13, 2010. http://nationalhumanitiescenter.org/pdsmaai/identity/text7/fleetwooddiary.pdf.

4 W. F. Beyer and O. F. Keydel, *Deeds of Valor: How America's Civil War Heroes Won the Congressional Medal of Honor* (New York: Smithmark, 2000), 434–435.

5 Ibid.

6 Congressional Medal of Honor Society, 2010. Accessed on July 5, 2010. http://www.cmohs.org/.

7 Charles Johnson Jr., National Park Service. October 3, 2007. Accessed on December 20, 2011. http://www.nps.gov/rich/historyculture/cfbio.htm.

8 Christian A. Fleetwood, "The Negro as Soldier," 1895. http://www.nps.gov/rich/historyculture/writings1.htm.

9 William J. Bennett, *America: The Last Best Hope* (Nashville: Thomas Nelson, 2006), 376.

10 Fleetwood, "Diary."

~ Five ~

PURPOSE, PERSPECTIVE, AND PRIDE

A ROYAL DILEMMA

It had only been a few days since he had last stood before this mass of people now assembled from every corner of the nation, but it felt like an eternity. Just three days ago, they had come together to set him in as their new king. But before doing so, they wanted to know just one thing: How would he rule over them? They said to him, "Your father made our yoke hard; now therefore lighten the hard service of your father and his heavy yoke which he put on us, and we will serve you."

With a greater inheritance awaiting him than had ever been amassed in the history of humanity (before or since), Rehoboam stood before the expectant crowd of people whom he was both prepared and determined to rule. Yet this demand that they brought before him was unexpected. They had caught him in a moment of uncertainty; never in his wildest dreams had he anticipated such a request.

His grandfather had been a mighty warrior who had fought and expanded his kingdom so effectively that his father had only seen peace during his entire reign. His father had been world-renowned for his just and wise decisions, so much so that kings and queens would travel from faraway nations just to hear him and bring him tribute. Now, after all this, after all that his family had done to build and establish this nation to the far reaches of the earth, how could these ungrateful people dare to make any demands on him before crowning him their new king?

Unprepared and unable to answer in that moment, he told them, "Come back to me in three days, and at that time I will give you my answer."

Distraught and rejected, Rehoboam did what all good kings were supposed to do—he sought out the advice of his late father's wisest and most trusted counselors. Upon hearing of his dilemma, they said to him, "If you will be a servant to this people today, and will serve them and grant them their petition, and speak good words to them, then they will be your servants forever" (1 Kings 12:7). Nevertheless, even though he knew their counsel was trustworthy and true, he found that it did not satisfy him, nor did it appeal to the strength and grandeur with which he intended to rule. He would not have his own subjects making demands of him!

Desperate to answer his subjects in such a way that would preserve his dignity and satisfy his concept of what it meant to be a legendary king, Rehoboam sought different advice—advice from the young men whom he had grown up with. Upon hearing of the ultimatum given by the people, his young friends became indignant on behalf of their childhood cohort and suggested a response that resonated in the heart of this future king. It confirmed for Rehoboam the type of king that he was destined to become, and it was the response that he was now prepared to give to those who stood before him.

As the people gathered and eventually quieted themselves in order to hear the response of this man whom they intended to set in as their new king, Rehoboam stepped forward and firmly said to them, "My little finger is thicker than my father's loins! Whereas my father loaded you with a heavy yoke, I will add to your yoke; my father disciplined you with whips, but I will discipline you with scorpions!" As a result, only two portions of his kingdom remained and received him as king, instead of the twelve that he was set to inherit on that day.[1]

Rehoboam was the son of King Solomon, of whom it was said that there was never a wiser man, before or since.[2] His mother was from a rival nation, and one among hundreds of wives whom his father had married.[3] Other than this, we know very little of his upbringing or his personal life. It's enough, however, that if we so desired, we *could* make a great many excuses for him and his mishandling of this situation. After all, when your father has seven hundred wives and over three hundred mistresses (and God only knows how many children), it's probably safe to assume that you might need a little psychological help. Yet the fact of the matter remains that, in this case at least, Rehoboam made a rather unwise choice. And while he might not have demonstrated the characteristic wisdom for which his father was so well-known, he does give us a story and an example from which much wisdom can still be gleaned.

PERSPECTIVE

To begin with, let's consider the very thing that Rehoboam sought out and needed most: counsel, or perspective. Perspective is simply our personal view or perception of an object or a situation. For many, perspective often boils down to this—opinion. Unfortunately, many Americans have developed a strong disdain for others' opinions, dismissing them with the commonly held belief that opinions are like the exit point for poop from the body—everyone has one, and they all stink. For many of us, we do not need to look any further than the dysfunction of our own federal government, with all of the "knowledgeable" politicians and their opinions, in order to seemingly prove our point. However, I encourage you to consider the fact that not all opinions or perspectives are created equal. In fact, I submit to you that there is opinion, and then there is perspective, and there *is* a difference between the two!

> *Opinion* is input or theory that is purely subjective, having little or no factual basis. *Perspective*, on the other hand, is input or theory that always has its roots in fact.

For example, let's say that a storm comes through and damages my home when I am out of town, and I ask for input about the damage from two different people: one who is standing right in front of my house and another who lives across town. The one who is standing right in front of my house can at least see a portion of it and is therefore in a position to give me rather valuable input into its status. What can the person across town give me? His opinion! He cannot even see my house, and so he would be a fool to venture any serious input. However, fools do exist. So we must do our best to differentiate between those who truly have a skilled or proper perspective, and those who are merely well-intentioned or may have ulterior motives in giving their opinion.

The guy across town can likely tell me how bad the storm was, perhaps having experienced the same storm himself, and he could even guess (give an opinion) as to what might have happened to my home. Yet the only real perspective he can give is as it relates to the storm itself. Still others may offer an opinion simply out of a desire to be needed and/or loved, but they have no real perspective, just an opinion for the sake of getting the attention they seek. It seems that Rehoboam had all of this at his fingertips, and yet he chose to go with opinion instead of perspective, for reasons that we will discuss shortly.

Solomon himself stated several times that wisdom can be found in a multitude of counselors.[4] So, the next question is this: How many counselors, or persons with perspective, do we truly need? Well, it depends on what you're looking at. Let's take our previous example. If I want to know the status of my home after a potentially damaging storm, I need at least one person who can see all sides of the house. But two or three people looking at the house would be even better, since we all tend to focus on different details of what we are looking at. Or, I could use four different people, each standing on different sides of the house and each giving their view or perception of my home. Would some of the perspectives be different? Yes, I would expect this, since they are all on different sides of the house, yet each is needed in order to get the fullest picture necessary to determine the status of my home.

My point is this: As long as I have people who are able to actually see my home, more perspectives will give a fuller picture of what's going on and allow me to make the best decision possible. Wisdom is truly found in a multitude of good counselors who are able to give proper perspective, in order that we might see the fullest possible picture of any given situation.

PURPOSE

Purpose is the intent, or *reason*, for which a certain thing is done. It is what drives us and keeps us going in a particular direction. It can be applied to any given task at hand, or it can be that which defines us in all that God has called us to do and to be in life. Purpose (or the lack thereof) often means the difference between thriving and withering, joy and depression, success and failure. In and of itself, purpose is neither good nor evil, but it is a necessary tool for the success of either one (though evil intent will always ultimately lead to failure). Purpose will always accompany great men and women, and it will always influence perspective.

Let us consider another example. Say I walk into a room with five different people and simply hand them a hammer and the materials needed for building a box, with no further instructions. Granted, each person has their own perspective about what I gave them, but no *purpose* was indicated. The result might look something like this:

Person #1 decides to pick up the hammer in order to build a box, while person #2 steps in to inquire if #1 is a part of the Carpenters Union, and is therefore qualified to use the hammer. Upon hearing what #2 is up to, #3 quickly jumps into action and drafts legislation that states that the hammer could never be handled safely by any person, union or not, without first attending a four-year training course conducted by the federal government, and advocates a special tax that would cover the cost of the training. Meanwhile, #1 is enraged by the fact that he should be required to be part of a union, and that he is not considered "safe enough" to use the hammer properly. He begins contemplating whether or not to use the hammer to bring about serious bodily harm to #2 and #3. Observing all of this, #4 is now upset and begins to march around the room with picket signs, advocating that the hammer should be left undisturbed in the place where it was originally placed, and he begins creating rock songs with really bad lyrics to be sung by terribly old and forgotten rock bands about how "disturbing" the original position of the hammer would most definitely ruin the beauty of the surrounding room. Upon seeing all of this, #5 becomes extremely frustrated with the whole situation and begins to pray that the hammer would just "will" itself to be used, and that "something" would be miraculously created whether someone actually picks up the hammer or not!

When purpose is not clearly communicated and defined, perspective runs amok and we wind up with a dysfunctional democracy. Purpose will *always* bring clarity to perspective.

Or consider a group of people that is asked to look at an empty field and tell you what they see. The answers will be broad and endless. However, take that same group of people and tell them that you are considering whether or not to buy that field in order to build a new home, and suddenly perspective becomes much more focused and useful. Now, go one step further and handpick your group of people to consist of contractors, architects, realtors, engineers, and land-scapers, then present them with the same purpose, and suddenly you've got a wealth of information to help you decide whether or not to buy the field. So not only will purpose give focus to perspective, but it will also assist you in identifying those from whom perspective is most needed.

Rehoboam had a purpose: to rule over the people with an iron fist and show them who was boss. And as for perspective, he had two sets of counselors. So, where did he go wrong?

PRIDE

Pride is nothing more than having a strong focus on self. *My* needs, *my* desires, *my* happiness, *my* kingdom! It is not the same as acknowledging that what God has made in creating me is good: Rather, it is that which goes beyond this understanding to the point that I become the sole focus of everything—otherwise known as self-worship.

Do a little experiment for me. (Hypothetically speaking, do not actually try this at home!) Grab a hand held mirror and begin staring intently at yourself, looking very closely at every last detail over and over. Now, imagine what would happen if you continued to do this while you walk to the busiest intersection in town—a large town like New York or Chicago in case you live in some small town like Genoa, Ohio—and crossed the street, back and forth for the next hour. Chances are you wouldn't survive past 30 seconds! That's pride. Pride goes before destruction.

Rehoboam might have had purpose, but unfortunately *he alone* was the main focus of his world. As a result, he sought out counsel that merely reinforced that focus. Have you ever gone to your friends or family supposedly looking for advice, but you didn't stop until you found someone to support the decision you had already made in your own mind? I have. That too is pride because it did not really matter what anyone else had to say. I did not even consider the opinions of the other people I talked to because I was so focused on what I wanted, what I needed, and what I desired. If this is the case, and pride can so utterly blind the best of us, how can we possibly guard ourselves against it?

HUMILITY

Humility is what Rehoboam required most in his hour of need. Humility allows us to acknowledge who we are and what we are called to do and to be, while placing our focus on *more* than just ourselves. Had he chosen to listen to his father's counselors, Rehoboam would have found that, in the process of focusing on the people's needs, he would also have fulfilled his own desire to be a great king. But instead, he sought out his own self-centered purpose, and thus he suffered the loss of over 80 percent of his intended kingdom in one day.

Humility, like everything else we've discussed in this book so far, involves choice. It is not a genetic trait, but a part of our character. If we choose not to pursue it, there's no need for us to read any further, for all that we have learned and begun to apply depends upon our ability to look past ourselves and consider those around us. True heroes would cease to exist, and trust would not be established if it weren't for the choice to put on humility. There is no harm in allowing our core values and beliefs to be challenged, but doing so requires humility. Either we discover that what we have is excellent, or we will find that it was not truly worth holding on to. In either case, humility is needed to seek out the proper perspective.

Pride is that most attractive set of glasses that creates the illusion that everything we say or do is correct. Removing a body part seems more acceptable than removing these glasses, yet we seldom see accurately with them on.

Pride and laziness have brought us to that place where the nation we once knew now hangs by a thread. If we are ever to step into the fullness of our calling as a nation, we must embrace humility so that we might once again see our purpose more clearly. As a nation, we have a purpose, and it begins as follows:

We the People of the United States, in Order to form a more perfect Union, establish Justice, insure domestic Tranquility, provide for the common defense, promote the general Welfare, and secure the Blessings of Liberty to ourselves and our Posterity, do ordain and establish this Constitution for the United States of America....[5]

It is from this purpose that we need to once again seek the proper perspective to assess where exactly we now stand, and where we need to go or return to as a nation. And it is for this purpose that we need to humble ourselves and look for the common ground that we share with one another before it's too late.

RECOMMENDED READING

1 Samuel, 2 Samuel, 1 Kings, 2 Kings
—Whether you're a seasoned reader of this wonderful book or scared to pick it up for fear that you'll be struck by lightning, these particular books of the Bible make wonderful reading. They tell the full story behind Rehoboam, Solomon, and David along with a few others. For the first time reader of this book, it reads easy and there's nothing to interpret, just good stories, history, and great life's lessons that continue to speak to us even today.

Notes

1 1 Kings 12:1–15 NASB

2 1 Kings 3:10–15 NASB

3 1 Kings 11:1–13; 14:21 NASB

4 Proverbs 11:14; 15:22; 20:18; 24:6 NASB

5 The United States Constitution.

~ Six ~

FORGIVENESS

Few occasions in recent history have so devastated and so galvanized the American people as the events of September 11, 2001. It was inconceivable that anyone could act with such cowardice and reckless abandon as was displayed by Muslim extremists on that day, stealing the lives of thousands in a vain attempt to terrorize our nation. Such hatred defies human comprehension, demands justice, and is nothing short of evil personified. Families were devastated, a city was torn apart, and a nation fell to its knees in mourning. Yet as the dust cleared in the days that followed, many stories of heroism, self-sacrifice, and courage emerged. Ever so slowly, the American people staggered to their feet, prepared themselves for war, and began searching for answers that defied explanation. As the nation rightly sought out justice and retribution, one woman discovered them more fully, and even unexpectedly, through the often-underutilized virtue of *forgiveness*.

9/11 NIGHTMARE

For Cheryl McGuinness, September 11, 2001, started like any other day. Her husband, Tom, kissed her good-bye on his way out the door to catch an early flight.[1] Tom had been a pilot for American Airlines for the past twelve years, and before that he had served for ten years in the U.S. Navy as an F-14 fighter pilot, having been honorably discharged at the rank of Lieutenant-Commander. He was one of the navy's finest, having attended the Top Gun training program, and Cheryl never worried about him when he went to work.[2]

A few hours after Tom had left, Cheryl found herself sitting on the back deck, enjoying the sun in the silence of the early morning. It was a great time to do her daily devotions and to reminisce. They had just celebrated Tom's forty-second birthday the night before with their children, and they'd had a wonderful time. Indeed, life was good. Cheryl was just about to update her journal about all the blessings the Lord had given them, when she heard the phone ring.[3] It was a good friend of theirs calling to see how she was doing, asking about Tom and his whereabouts that day. As it turned out, it was the first of many calls she would receive that morning from close friends asking the same questions. Eventually one of them told her that a plane had been hijacked and that she needed to turn on the television.

She immediately tried to contact Tom by phone and then by his pager, but there was no response from either one. Finally, after several other unsuccessful attempts to find answers, a black car pulled up to the house and several men in dark suits came to the door. They informed Cheryl that Tom had been the copilot on American Airlines Flight 11, which had been hijacked and crashed into the World Trade Center in New York City, and that, unfortunately, there were no survivors.[4]

Tom and Cheryl had celebrated their eighteenth wedding

anniversary just a few weeks before. On that night, Tom had told her of a close friend who was now in a coma following a bad car accident that had also killed his wife instantly. They talked about death and had discussed the possibility of dealing with Tom's loss should anything ever happen to him unexpectedly. Cheryl wasn't sure she was strong enough to endure the pain of such a loss, and she had even told him that as they'd talked. However, Tom had reassured her that night that while she was not strong enough, God was. He had told her, "Trust God, and He will get you through it."[5] Nevertheless, nothing could have prepared her for the shock and utter devastation of the news that was now before her. The love of her life had just been ripped from her mercilessly, and her children were now fatherless. As was the case with most Americans on that day, there was no way to fully comprehend what had just taken place. There was only pain, disbelief, and an overwhelming sense of loss.

Nearly a year later, Cheryl visited Ground Zero for the first time. All that remained of the Twin Towers was an enormous pit where they once stood. Overwhelmed, she slowly began to examine the barren and disquieting landscape that now lay before her. As she did so, her eyes fell upon a cross, the only steel structure that remained standing. Defying all human logic, she knew in that moment that God was asking her to forgive the terrorists who had perpetrated this unspeakable crime. *Forgive them.* Cheryl wrestled with this thought, asking God *why* she should forgive them, and saying to Him, "Lord, they killed my husband!" But God's response to her was simply this: *"Because I forgave you."* She did not exactly want to, but from that point on, Cheryl made a commitment to actively forgive them for what they had done to her, to Tom, to her children, and to the nation. It was not easy, but as a result, her perspective grew and released her to begin focusing on others again and moving upon all of the things that she knew God was calling her to do and to be. Forgiveness allowed her to release her husband's killers to God and to trust in His justice.[6]

JUSTICE AND FORGIVENESS

Of all that we have discussed in this book thus far, the concept of forgiveness is perhaps the most elusive and poorly understood. For many people, the thought of forgiveness carries with it the connotation of being fake with someone who has deeply wronged us, so that we don't rock the boat. We've come to believe that forgiveness is letting people "off the hook," or that it simply requires saying "I'm sorry" when we've wronged others. In essence, many Americans have come to equate forgiveness with injustice, believing that the concepts of justice and forgiveness do not and can not possibly exist together. However, the truth of the matter is this: *True justice cannot exist without forgiveness.*

Justice itself is another poorly understood concept. In short, it means to weigh out with equity (impartially or with fairness). It is often portrayed as a balance scale that requires equal amounts of weight to be placed on each side in order to maintain a balance. In the natural realm it means that if I pay for ten pounds of apples, I had better receive 10 pounds of apples—balanced scales—I get what I pay for. In the realm of human behavior, it is no different: We desire "just" rewards for good behavior, and "just" punishment for bad behavior.

However, in the realm of behavior, especially bad behavior it does not seem like these same rules apply. For example, let's say that someone purposefully and brutally takes the life of the person whom you are closest to right now. What is just or fair in this situation? How many years should they serve in prison? Should they die for their crime? You make the call. Carry out the punishment. Now, does it make you feel any better? For most of us, even if we choose the harshest sentence possible, our justice is only partial at best. Why? Because while the person who committed the act might suffer greatly for their crime, it still does not replace the very thing that we have been deprived of and long for the most: our relationship with the person who has been lost.

In fact, no matter how hard you may try, justice cannot be served in full. No scales can fully weigh out and reward you with what you desire and deserve most: to have your loved one returned to you. To focus on this aspect alone often leaves us empty, bitter, and unfulfilled, regardless of the punishment. Until forgiveness is applied, justice remains incomplete at best. *Forgiveness* means "to lift" another person's sins or transgressions.[7] But lift it where? To the only One who can ever establish true justice and turn inequitable situations in our favor.

There is no human court on the face of this earth that could ever grant us the justice we so often desire—and even deserve—when we are wronged. Thankfully, through forgiveness, there is another court to which we can appeal. If you are experiencing a bitter loss, this may sound totally convoluted, so let me explain.

TRUE FORGIVENESS

Forgiveness is simply refusing to make yourself

someone's judge and jury for a past sin, hurt, or offense; it is choosing to release the offender to God's judgment instead. (This does not mean we are letting them off the hook; again, bear with me as I explain.) When we choose to forgive, we are simply stepping out of the way so that God can deal with that person more fully.[8]

And because we are stepping out of the way, we also find that we become free to focus on the people and things that really matter again. No longer do we need to focus on the loss or the bitterness of injustice because we have assurance that one day, whether we see it in this lifetime or not, true justice will be served.

Conversely, when we choose *not* to forgive, not only do we lose that which has already been stolen from us, but we also lose our ability to move beyond the pain and therefore we surrender our future (and perhaps the best of our days) to the very person who has already stolen so much from us. In spite of the potential hurt or anger we may feel over an offense, choosing not to forgive is no more than *choosing to focus on yourself and your misery*, which in the end will always leave you *by yourself, with your misery*.

Now, because this concept has been so misused and misunderstood throughout the years, it is also necessary to review what forgiveness *is not*. Many of you may agree in concept with the above statements on forgiveness, yet you find it difficult to apply them due to personal experience or other teachings on forgiveness. So, let's destroy some of the most common lies about forgiveness:

FORGIVENESS IS NOT...[9]

1. **Approving what the offender did.** Forgiveness is quite

the opposite; it is acknowledging that what someone else did *was* wrong, but choosing to release them to God's justice instead of our own.

2. **Excusing what the offender did.** There is no excuse for sin (those things that others have done to us that are definitely wrong). Yet we may find that some offenses (those things that *offend* us, but that *may* or *may not* be definitively "wrong"), whether *real* or *perceived*, are oftentimes more the result of miscommunication and misunderstanding. We need to discern the difference and, in some cases, be willing to talk things out with the offender to determine their intent.

3. **Justifying what the offender did.** Forgiving/releasing them does not justify (make right) what someone has said or done; it merely releases you from being their judge and jury and frees you from being "bound," or limited, by their offense.

4. **Pardoning what the offender did.** We can forgive, yet we can still be involved in the process to help hold people accountable. Cheryl McGuinness was able to forgive the terrorists, yet she did not believe for one minute that meant they should go free and unpunished for their crimes. Again, she simply removed herself from being their judge and jury. However, there are instances when we can and even should decide to show mercy and pardon an offender. We *do* reap what we sow.

5. **Reconciliation with an offender (reestablishing a good relationship).** This *may* happen, but it is not necessary in order for us to forgive.

6. **Denying what the offender did.** Forgiveness *requires* an

acknowledgment of the offense. *Denial*, whether consciously or subconsciously, is for those who choose not to deal with the problem and therefore remain bound, or limited, by an offense. They will continue to be bound until they can acknowledge it, deal with it, forgive it, and move on.

7. **Turning a blind eye to what happened.** *Denial* is choosing to turn a blind eye to what happened (the truth). *Forgiveness* acknowledges what happened and brings it into the light to be dealt with.

8. **Forgetting what the offender did.** People often speak of "forgiving and forgetting"—but this simply means that once we have forgiven an individual for an offense, we choose not to punish them in our *present* interactions for something that took place in the *past*. However, on this side of heaven we may never forget what someone did to us or to our loved ones, and *at times* it's even appropriate that we *should not*. For example, we can forgive "former" child molesters and not punish them for their past sins as we interact with them in the present, but this does not mean we should forget what they did or leave our children in their care.

9. **Refusing to take the offense seriously.** On the contrary, offering true forgiveness requires that we take the time to carefully consider the seriousness of a matter.

10. **Pretending we are not hurt by the offense.** Forgiveness does not necessitate that we feel a certain way toward the one who offended us; it is simply a choice we make (regardless of and independent from our feelings) in order to obtain true justice.(5)

As mentioned in this list, offenses can be real or perceived. There are times when people truly do wrong us by what they do or say. And then there are times when it's a matter of what we perceived they've said or done. When we fail to distinguish between real and perceived offenses, it can lead to the unnecessary loss of a close friend or ally. As long as the world contains people, however, some of them will wrong us, and there is nothing we can do about it other than to forgive them.

This chapter is by no means a definitive work on forgiveness. In fact, there is much more that can and even should be shared in order to understand the full scope of forgiveness and its ramifications. It is important to both consider and apply forgiveness in our daily lives if we are to effectively find and willingly step into our common ground.

Forgiveness is a vital component of freedom and justice. It is a choice that can be made regardless of our feelings, and it does not necessitate the removal of consequences.

Forgiveness is one of the hallmarks of the *hero*. For those instances when we may or may not have the full story, we must seek the proper *perspective* in order to determine whether we were truly wronged or are simply suffering from a case of misunderstanding or miscommunication. Unforgiveness keeps us from stepping into the fullness of all that God has for us and desires to work through us (our *purpose*). It often keeps us from *trusting* and partnering with a great number of good people—including God Himself. Does God need our forgiveness? No, but we often blame Him for things that are not His doing. Therefore, in order to gain a proper perspective, we do need to release Him and "forgive"

Him, as well. This allows us to see Him more clearly for who He is and understand that His intentions for us are nothing but good in spite of what we may have been led to believe about Him. He is no different from anyone else we've discussed so far: If we've got a problem with Him, we need to discuss it with Him. If we believe He's wronged us, we need to go to the Source to see if what we are believing is, in fact, true.

It's not politically correct to talk about God these days, yet on 9/11 we turned to Him as a nation, as we so often do in times of crisis. He is the foundation of our freedom, and forgiveness has a key role to play in it, for those who choose to avail themselves of it. I find it both interesting and ironic that in the process of declaring our *independence* "with a firm reliance upon the protection of Divine Providence...,"[10] we were also declaring our *dependence* upon God. He is so much more than a swear word or a crisis intervention manager. If we are to move forward as a nation, we must understand and acknowledge the role He has played and still desires to play in our country. Our freedom is an integral part of His sovereignty. We must also comprehend more fully that the God of the universe is *real*, *tangible*, and *evident*; His words are not limited to an old book that sits on the nightstand and collects dust. If we are to move forward in finding our common ground, and in seeing this nation move and operate in the fullness of her original mandate, we must go beyond merely calling out to Him in times of crisis and learn once again how to *listen*.

RECOMMENDED READING

John and Paula Sanford, and Lee Bowman, *Choosing Forgiveness*, 2003.

—For the reader struggling to apply forgiveness, this is a very good and comprehensive source. Otherwise, I would suggest you check out the appendix in the back of this book.

Notes

1 The 700 Club. 2010. Accessed May 18, 2010. http://www.cbn.com/700club/guests/bios/cheryl_mcguinness_090904.aspx.

2 Anne M. Mozingo, *Portsmouth Herald*, December 23, 2001. Accessed on May 18, 2010. http://archive.seacoastonlie.com/2001news/12_23b.htm.

3 Ibid.

4 *The 700 Club.*

5 Mozingo.

6 *The 700 Club*; Mozingo.

7 James Strong, *Strong's Hebrew and Greek Dictionary*, 2003, H5375.

8 Isaiah 54:17 NASB

9 R. T. Kendall, *Total Forgiveness* (Lake Mary, FL: Charisma House, 2002), only bolded portion in the list are from the source.

10 The Declaration of Independence.

~ Seven ~

A REVOLUTIONARY POINT OF VIEW

I did not consider it any part of my charge to invent new Ideas, but to place before mankind the common sense of the subject, in terms so plain and firm as to command their assent. —*Thomas Jefferson*

I could not have said it any better. It is not my purpose in writing this book to prove or invent, but to merely present for your consideration a small sampling of key components that impact this nation's past and present for the purpose of helping us to move forward into our God-given destiny. To that end, we cannot go much further without taking into account Divine Providence (aka God) and His involvement in a free nation. Others have compiled overwhelming evidence of His influence and involvement by clearly presenting legal documents, diaries, letters, and more, that state the intentions of our Founders on this matter. (See recommended reading lists.) Yet for my part, I simply desire to add a little common-sense perspective while at the same time challenging you to think outside of the box that we have attempted to keep Him in for far too long.

A CHRISTIAN NATION?

Are we a Christian nation? We are a nation founded upon biblical values that has declared our dependence upon the Judeo-Christian God, and we are one in which the vast majority of Americans continue to at least profess some form of Christianity as the core of their faith. Conservatively, over 75 percent and possibly as many as 92 percent of Americans are professing or active Christians, based on Gallup Poll data compiled in 2008, 2009, and again at the end of 2015.[1] In this sense, we are, indeed, a Christian nation.

Therefore, the next question is this: Does being a Christian nation in this sense pose a threat to the non-Christian? Absolutely not. First of all, the First Amendment to our Constitution ensures the rights of the non-believers every bit as much as those of believers. No one is or ever shall be forced into any type of religion or non-religion, so long as we hold to the integrity of this document. Second, the true God of the Bible that the Christian serves does not *demand* acceptance or submission and in no way seeks to limit our freedom in any way, shape, or form. He knows that love cannot be programmed into us like a computer, but that it must be freely given in order to have any value. From the beginning, we were given a choice to accept or reject Him, and because of this, the freedom of all humanity is of the utmost importance to Him. So greatly does He value our liberty that He even gave us boundaries that would, if followed, safeguard those liberties. Consider:

"Thou shall not kill"—protection of self.
"Thou shall not steal"—protection of personal
    property.

"Thou shall not commit adultery"—protection of
   relationships.

These are nothing more than the values that we find un-
dergirding our Constitution, and they are no less than those
that were spoken of in our Declaration of Independence:

We hold these truths to be self-evident, that all men
are created equal, that they are endowed by their
Creator with certain unalienable Rights, that among
these are Life, Liberty and the pursuit of Happiness.

It was self-evident (that is, obvious, undeniable, indis-
putable) to our Founders that we were given these rights, and
it was self-evident that they were given to us by God.

SO WHAT, AND WHO CARES?

As a result of having declared our reliance upon Him, it is
only logical then that we should need to communicate and interact with the One in whom we trust and upon whom rely.
Would you depend upon your attorney if all you ever did was
talk to him and give him your input, without getting his advice in return? Absurd, right? If we are going to depend upon
someone, then we need their input, direction, and feedback;
we need to know them well enough to trust them. In short,
we need to be able to hear their voice. As Christians, we
serve a God who offers no less. Not only are we able to talk
to Him, we are also able to hear His voice.[2] God speaks to
both the believer and the non-believer alike, if they would
choose to listen. In fact, this book was written for one simple
reason—because one night, while I was sitting in my living
room praying (communicating, speaking, and listening to

74

God), He told me to write it. Now, if someone had told me I'd be writing a book before God spoke to me about it, I would have laughed and listed a number of reasons why I was the least-qualified candidate to ever be writing a book. However, when God speaks, the unqualified become qualified, the unbelievable becomes believable, life changes…and so do you.

> A word from a friend is helpful, but a word from the Living God will rock you to your core; you will not remain unchanged.

Aside from telling me to write it, He also spoke to me that night of things that He desired to impart through me to the nation—to the believer and unbeliever alike. What follows is just the first half of that word. It was given for you, the reader, regardless of your station in life, and it was given to this nation to help continue what He has already begun through others: a *rekindling of the spirit of revolution.*

A WORD FROM THE LIVING GOD—PART I

My beloved people, you have captured My heart from the inception of your nation. You have been from the beginning and remain a people of passion, purpose, and destiny. Though spiritually you have fallen asleep, My love for you remains as strong as ever. I have also watched as some who serve Me and some who would claim to serve Me have risen up in their own strength to serve their own selfish ends. Those in leadership, both political and that of My Church, have abused their power and injured many. But what grieves Me the most is how this has fractured and divided My Church, wounding and abandoning thousands upon thousands in the process, and causing many to turn their backs on Me entirely.

My Church has left her original mandate, and many have just cause to look on her in scorn and disappointment... But where many have failed, there are still those who have remained faithful, and they can be found across every dividing line that is within My Church. I have heard their cries, and the cry of the lost, of the hurting, and especially of those who have been injured in any way by My Church...and I ask your forgiveness on behalf of those who misrepresented Me to you. I have seen and collected every tear that you've cried as a result of the abuse and pain that My Church has caused you through the years. Please know, My child, that it was not I who abused you, for in My love for you I desire nothing but blessing upon blessing.

And know too that the cleansing of My house has already begun, and it will continue to increase in the coming years. I have shown great mercy and compassion to My Church, and I have given many of those in her leadership time to repent and change their ways. But for the sake of My people, their time draws short; and if they do not repent, they will continue to be removed. My people have prayed that I would cleanse this nation and heal this land, and this I am both doing and about to do in ways that will become increasingly visible. But in order to cleanse your nation, I must first start with My own household. I will continue to remove the hirelings throughout My Church, and it will become much more difficult for them to pose as something they are not.

For the light shall continue to grow ever brighter, and the darkness ever deeper. Discernment between good and evil will greatly increase, and not just inside of My Church, but outside of her, as well, as people begin to perceive and acknowledge My Word, which I have written upon their hearts. This will happen because I have poured out My Spirit upon all flesh and not just the few elect.

Evil will not simply disappear, but rather it will begin to be exposed for what it truly is, much sooner and much more easily than before. The righteous will begin to stand up for what is right and what is good in greater and greater numbers. This groundswell of holy righteousness will begin through acts of selflessness and self-sacrifice, as men and women put reputations, political careers, public standing, popularity, financial gain, and even their very lives on the line in some instances, in order to stand up for what is right and for what is good.

What has begun in small pockets will swell up into a wave of holy righteousness that will sweep across the nation and touch every level of social, political, and religious life and activity. It will be a time of renewing and mending of the nets. Connections will be established across various denominational, racial, societal, and political lines, in order to prepare for what is yet to come.

Before true revival can take place, My Church must first be restored, find her identity, and begin operating within her true purpose and authority. The days of pew-sitting are drawing to an end. For men and women will either be drawn to engage, or they will fall away. Sitting on the fence will no longer be an option. I am much more than what many have come to know of Me.

Many have sat back and fallen into a coma of boredom, thinking that this [pew-sitting] is what Christians do, and that this is fulfilling what I want them to do. I do not require that you merely come to church, and you do not become a better person or more acceptable to Me by doing so. I desire to know you, to have a relationship with you, and you with My people, as I dwell in them and in you. If you are going to church to impress Me or others—STOP! Don't try to impress Me—talk to Me, listen to what I have to say to you—spend time with Me and know the depth, the height, the vastness of My love for you.

Begin to know the purpose for which I created you and called you. Yes, called YOU! I have not just called the pastors, the priests, and the leaders; I have called every one of you by name, and each one of you has a purpose, a calling, and gifts that I have given, or will give, in order to fulfill what I have called you to do and to be. Press into Me; press into My people!

DO NOT STOP TRUSTING simply because some have taken My name and used it for their own purposes. I am deeply grieved when I see those whom I have truly called, abusing and using others for their own ends, to serve their own needs. Make no mistake—justice will be served in the end for those who would do this and severely if they do not repent. But know too that even these I love, and I desire for them to walk in the fullness of what I have called them to do and to be—not what they have shown you in their foolishness. I beg of you to forgive them and not to judge Me based upon how you have been treated by the wolves, the thieves, or some of the misguided and severely injured shepherds in My Church.

I AM safe! And I AM worthy of your trust like no other! I have and will continue to raise up even more godly men and women of character and integrity whom you can trust and in whom you can find safety and restoration...

RECOMMENDED READING

1. Mark and Patti Virkler, *Dialogue with GOD: Opening the Door to Two-Way Prayer*, 2005.

—This is an absolutely wonderful book whether you are a new believer, a veteran of the faith, or simply curious about this whole "Christianity thing" and what it means to hear God's voice. Easy to read and deeply rooted in Scripture, this book will challenge you to the core. Good stuff!

2. Harold R. Eberle, *Christianity Unshackled: Are You a Truth Seeker?* 2009.

—Okay, yes, I mentioned this book at the end of chapter two, but it has significant application for the content of this chapter as well. Once again, this is an excellent book for the reader who needs to search things out a bit deeper, but who desires a resource that's easy to read, historically accurate, and yet holds nothing back.

In need of personal assistance? Once again I would direct you to the appendix in the back of this book.

Notes

1 Frank Newport, "Easter Season Finds a Religious, Largely Christian, Nation," *Gallup,* March 21, 2008. Accessed on June 11, 2010. http://www.gallup.com/poll/105544/Easter-Season-Finds-Religious-Largely-Christian-Nation.aspx; Frank Newport, "This Christmas, 78% of Americans Identify as Christian," Gallup, December 24, 2009. Accessed on January 7, 2012. http://www.gallup.com/poll/124793/This-Christmas-78-Americans-Identify-Christian.aspx; Frank Newport, "Percentage of Christians in U.S. Drifting Down, but Still High," *Gallup*, December 24, 2015.

2 John 10:27 NASB

Part Two

Rebuilding Ancient Foundations, aka Our Common Ground

Those from among you will rebuild the ancient ruins; you will raise up the age-old foundations; and you will be called the repairer of the breach, the restorer of the streets in which to dwell. —Isaiah 58:12 NASB

Eight

FOUNDER'S FOUNDERS

If we truly desire to begin a work of restoration, it's important that we begin our work from the ground up. Otherwise we may end up redoing work that we have already done and at a greater cost than necessary. The restoration of a nation is no different. It is important that we look at *what* the foundation truly is before we decide whether to rebuild, patch, or just keep building on top of it. To make this assessment, we need to inspect what is already there and attempt to discover *why* it was put there in the first place. This is the purpose and focus of the remaining chapters in this book. Another way of looking at it is this: The floor upon which we stand is the ceiling of those who have gone before us. In other words, each successive generation has the opportunity to build upon the achievements of the former generations and then go even higher. This is our starting point, as it was *also* the starting point of our Founding Fathers.

FAITH AND ACTION

A contemporary of Benjamin Franklin, young Jonny was born on October 5, 1703, in East Windsor, Connecticut. Both were born into strong Puritan[1] families whose heart's desires were to see their children succeed in life. Of further interest is that the fathers in each family sought to point their sons toward a life of ministry. And while on the surface it would appear that only one of them succeeded, I would contend that perhaps history tells a different story.

Ben's father was a very godly and devout tradesman, a candle maker, to be exact, and he had always hoped that this brilliant young son of his might one day pursue a life devoted to God. However, one of seventeen children born to Josiah Franklin, young Ben found the "long and repetitious family prayers to be boring" and impractical. For instance, it made no sense to Ben why one would pray over salted fish every time it was served instead of just blessing "the whole cask of salted fish at once" and being done with it. In spite of Ben's more practical rather than "pious" view of things, his father desired that he move in the direction of the ministry, and he proceeded to enroll him in Latin school. Unfortunately, Ben would have to withdraw after only one year due to financial strains on the family. He continued his education by reading every book he could get his hands on. While Ben had also entertained thoughts of life on the high seas, eventually Josiah encouraged him to apprentice with his brother James, who was setting up a printing press in Boston, a move that was not only much safer, but one that would propel him into a niche where he would absolutely flourish.

Jonny grew up in a similar home atmosphere as that of Ben. And while the expression of Ben's faith and his religious upbringing was shown forth in very practical and even quite extravagant ways (though some would argue that he later abandoned his Christian roots), Jonny's path lay within the Church. While most boys were out building a fort in the woods in which to play and fight imaginary Indians, Jonny built one with the sole intent and purpose of prayer with his young friends. At the age of nine, young Jonny was secretly praying five times a day, talking to his friends about God, and organizing prayer meetings for the other boys. While normal play and roughhousing might appeal to most of his young friends, Jonny was nothing like them. Nature was the one thing that could compete with God in his mind and even that only for a time.[3]

He loved "the outdoors—the countryside, the seashore, and all of nature." He said to himself, "Sometimes on fair days I find myself more particularly disposed to regard the glories of the world than to [engage] myself to the study of serious religion." Of particular interest were his study and observation of insects. While this was not entirely unusual for a young boy, Jonny went beyond catching them, pulling off their legs, and chasing unsuspecting little girls with them. Instead he took to writing down his observations of these marvelous little creatures, and at the age of eleven, he completed one of many such writings on nature, entitled "Of Insects."[4]

Born to Timothy and Esther Edwards, Jonny was one of eleven children and the only boy. His father, a traveling minister, loved to tell people that he had "sixty feet of daughters," as all of their children were unusually tall. Both parents were very well-educated and wonderful teachers, so it was only natural that the children's education began at home. Eventually all but one of Jonny's sisters would be sent to Boston for finishing school, which was certainly extraordinary in light of the fact that most young women of this time period were not encouraged to pursue anything beyond an elementary education. As a result, Jonny became the beneficiary of all of this, as he was not only tutored by his father and mother, but by his older sisters as well. No less brilliant than Ben, Jonny was eventually enrolled in what would later become known as Yale University at the age of thirteen.

The common tie? To be honest there were many, though it is doubtful that the two ever met. But of greatest interest was an event known to most as the Great Awakening,[6] which took place in the late 1730s and early 1740s. And while Franklin would go on to chronicle many of the events that unfolded in the *Pennsylvania Gazette* and he became lifelong friends with George Whitfield (another of the Awakening's key figures), many credit young Jonny, or Jonathan Edwards, as being one of the primary individuals whom God used to get the whole thing started.[7]

Why is this of interest? In a nutshell, the Great Awakening was a time of spiritual revival and renewal in which many people of the American colonies came to faith, or rather had personal encounters with the living God. What was once viewed as a dead religion to some, or the "folly of the weak-minded" to others, suddenly came alive, as multitudes began to have an experience with the God of the universe, which quite frankly rocked their world! Along with the obvious influences to our nation's Declaration of Independence and the Constitution (some of which we'll discuss later on), this spiritual awakening laid the groundwork that enabled people to embrace the very *idea* of a free and independent nation. Let me explain.

There were many theological thoughts and streams emerging during this time period as a result of someone in "authority, challenging authority." Yet, while the primary focus of this awakening was a close encounter with God, an unexpected but necessary outcome was the introduction of the thought that it was acceptable for the common person to challenge pastors who were not sufficiently spiritual. Therefore it was this key "principle of democracy—the authority of the common people" that came to be realized *first* in this spiritual revolution, long before it took center stage in the politics of the American Revolution. Indeed, Jonathan Edwards, George Whitfield, and their fellow counterparts who were used of God during the Great Awakening helped to lay the groundwork upon which our Founding Fathers stood.[8] And while Edwards might not be solely responsible for all of the good that came forth as a result of the Great Awakening (much of which we have only scratched the surface of, by the way), he *is* an excellent example of how the power of family can change the course of a nation.

THE POWER OF FAMILY

William Ross Wallace once wrote a poem entitled "The Hand That Rocks the Cradle Is the Hand That Rules the World." Originally published in 1865 under the title "What Rules the World," Wallace paid tribute to mothers as the primary, yet unsung source for change in the world. It's a lovely poem to be sure, and mothers everywhere have my deepest heartfelt gratitude and respect for all that they do. However, inasmuch as I believe that mothers do possess a great force for world change, I am here to remind you that there is a force that is infinitely more powerful—FAMILY!

For decades now, if not centuries, women have fought to earn their place in society, to be afforded the same rights, respect, and honor as men in this American culture and around the world. And just to be clear—this is not an attempt to squash, belittle, or trivialize what has been a hard-fought battle. The influence of a loving mother equipping, nurturing, and providing direction for her children is invaluable. Yet equally as powerful is the influence of a daddy in the life of a young child. Oh, to be certain it is not the same thing as what a mother gives—I'm the daddy of three, I totally understand! Love is expressed totally differently through a daddy and it generally looks more goofy and dangerous! But yet, that is what makes it so powerful and so invaluable—each parent has something unique to impart to a child, and without the influence of both, there *will* be something missing.

To go a step further, we need to understand that dads and moms come in all sorts of shapes, sizes, and temperaments, with different gifts, abilities, and personalities. We don't need to look like the mom or dad next door who may *seem* to have it all together. We simply need to parent the way God chose to express His love through us—*that* is what our children need! Can we be a single parent or be raised in a single-parent home and still have things turn out fine? Sure, God can fill the gap in any circumstance if we allow Him to do so. Death, divorce, gross acts of "foolishness" happen; I get it. But just because they happen does not mean that they are God's best for us and for future generations, or without consequences.

The Edwards family provides us with a stellar example of this. They do not *look* like the family next door. They were most certainly larger than the average family in both height and number, and Jonathan was anything but the typical young boy. But his family (his mother, his father, and all ten of his sisters) were exactly what *he* needed to fulfill all that God was calling him to do and to be in life. Every last one of them contributed to his life, helping to mold and shape him. Proverbs 22:6 says it like this: "Train up a child in the way he should go, even when he is old he will not depart from it." For the longest time, I thought this meant that if I would raise a child up the "right way," doing all the "right things," then they would not stray from doing the "right things." While there may be some truth to that, this verse literally says to raise children up "in their way"—in the way *they* should go! We *do* need to raise our children to do what is right and good, to love and respect others, etc. However, all of this is to equip them to walk in *their* specific gifts and abilities, not necessarily push them into what *we* think they should do or be.

This is challenging for many parents, because every last one of us usually has some great idea of what we want our children to grow up to do or to be, even before they are born. And sometimes we do know beforehand. Regardless of what that might be, it is our job as parents to help them discover what it is and then point, encourage, and equip them to go "in *their* way." Ben's family also did a great job at this. Did you notice that Josiah desired the same path as Edwards did for his young son? Yet, after taking some steps in that direction and discovering that this was not the right path for him, he helped his son regroup. Josiah Franklin may not have nailed it on the first try, but eventually, like Timothy and Esther Edwards, he was able to not only assist, but to propel his young son into a destiny that shook nations. That's the power of family!

HERITAGE

When we "do family" right, there is yet another benefit—we are able to leave a legacy, or a heritage, that will affect the world for generations to come. For example, while Timothy and Esther Edwards's primary focus might have been raising godly young children to help affect the world around them, it also produced a staggeringly rich heritage. The known descendants of Jonathan Edwards alone include:

- 13 college presidents
- 65 college professors
- 30 judges
- 100 lawyers, including the dean of an outstanding law school
- 66 physicians, including the dean of a medical school
- 75 army and navy officers
- 100 pastors
- 60 authors of prominence
- 3 United States senators
- 80 public servants in other capacities, including governors and ministers to foreign countries, and one vice president of the United States
- plus scores of college graduates, ministers, missionaries, prominent businessmen, authors, and editors[9]

Indeed, the power of family can change the course of the world in ways that are both seen and in ways that often times go unnoticed. Nonetheless our heritage is not derived solely from what can be found in recorded history—it is derived from what we choose to do with the time and resources that are available to us. If, at the end of the day, we've done our best and given it our all, we will have a legacy to be proud of, whether we see it in our lifetimes or not.

Some of you may be saying at this point, "Well, that's all

fine and good, but I have not done a good job at any of this, and my family is in shambles." Well, thank God for those who are in the business of restoration!

RESTORING THE POWER OF FAMILY

In June 2015, I had the privilege of meeting the Claussen family. They are, in my opinion, one of the most extraordinary and unique families on the face of the earth, hands down. Why? Because they carry the message of family in a way that few currently do, and at a time when this nation, if not the world, desperately needs it.

Dr. Jonathan and Amy Claussen have eight wonderful children—Jacob, Emma, Ben, Lydia, Maggie, Elijah, Silas, and Sadie! Their ministry? The Family Restoration Project! Traveling the country in a large motorhome, this family, including both of Jon and Amy's parents, share a message of real hope that families can *indeed* be restored and rebuilt. Their message is centered around restoring a proper loving relationship first and foremost with a loving God, and then infusing that love to bring restoration to the nuclear family. While many focus on unity across racial lines, political lines, etc., Jon and Amy desire the same, but they seek to accomplish it from a different starting point. As Jonathan writes in his book, *Restoring the Power of Family*, there is "no greater demonstration [of unity] on the earth…than the nuclear family" (nuclear family, meaning father, mother, children). He continues:

> If family is nuclear, it will have tremendous influence, either positively or negatively. If family operates outside of unity—if there is no peace and a lack of

honor—then the nuclear family is the greatest weapon of mass destruction known to man. When the nuclear family is authentic, unified, peaceful, and honoring, it is the greatest weapon of "mass affection." Family needs to be the greatest demonstration of love and compassion on the earth, first inwardly and then outwardly.

A family infused with this love, honor, and unity will not easily be divided. And if they truly understand what they have and are able to "do family" correctly, it will impact those around them in much the same way as the Edwards family.[10]

A STARTING POINT

So, what are some practical steps that we can take to help build and restore the family? One of the simplest is to purpose to spend time together. For the Claussens, it began with a period of time in which God encouraged them to play football and board games together, while setting other things aside. And while football had yet to be invented in Jonathan Edwards's day, the plan God gave to him for his family was very similar:

In no area was Edwards' resolve stronger than in his role as a father. Edwards and his wife, Sarah, had eleven children. Despite a rigorous work schedule that included rising as early as 4:30 a.m. to read and write in his library, extensive travels, and endless administrative meetings, he always made time for his children. Indeed, he committed to spending at least one hour a day with them. And what if he missed a day because he was traveling? He diligently made up the hour when he returned.[11]

This step will look different for each family. For us, it has included card games, music, and even cooking together. It may need to start with forgiveness before you can go any further—if so, then do it. Life is too short, and at the end of the day, there really is no valid excuse not to forgive. Difficult? Likely! But remember, it is for *your* freedom, and this process doesn't stand a chance without it. Whether you are a son, a daughter, or a parent with a family of your own—it is never too late in life to begin the process of family restoration!

I would highly recommend Dr. Claussen's book as a starting point for this journey, but the most important thing is simply that you start. Do not let the conviction to act go for so long that it just turns into another good idea that you will do when you "get around to it." Pray, act, and seek out help for the process. Yes, I said to *pray*. Listen, by now you have obviously figured out the core of my belief system and you decided to keep reading anyway. So, if you are a believer—pray. If you are not—take a chance and pray anyway. I love Him dearly and know of His goodness through my own experiences with Him, but if you have no such experience—I encourage you to take a chance. You just might be in for the surprise of your life and end up having a "great awakening" of your own!

Regardless, the restoration of the nuclear family in this nation has indeed begun, thanks to people like the Claussens and countless others who work to this end in both the religious and secular arenas. And it is essential that this continue as we seek to equip, encourage, and launch future generations into their God-given destinies, allowing them to pursue what many in this nation appear to be giving up on—the American dream.

RECOMMENDED READING

Jonathan Claussen, MD. *Restoring the Power of Family*. Bloomington, IN: WestBow Press, 2014.

—I do not think that anything further needs to be said. I highly recommend this book, and this family, to you.

Notes

1 The Puritans themselves were simply those of the Protestant religion who desired the government of England to hold to what *they* believed was the purest form of Protestantism, and not a form that adhered to the Protestant ideology while at the same time embracing the trappings and traditions of the Roman Catholics. Nevertheless, it became clear that they were in the minority by the late seventeenth century, and they soon found themselves less than welcome in England. Therefore many sought to make a new life in a new land; George M. Marsden, *A Short Life of Jonathan Edwards* (Grand Rapids: Eerdman's, 2008), Location 222.

2 Marsden, *A Short Life*, Location 222; James Baldwin, 2011. Accessed February 17, 2016. http://www.readbookonline.net/readOnLine/9372/.

3 Marsden, *A Short Life*, Location 225; Marsden, *Jonathan Edwards: A Life* (New Haven: Yale University Press, 2003), Location 421; Elizabeth D. Dodds, *Marriage to a Difficult Man* (Philadelphia: The Westminster Press, 1971), 38.

4 Elizabeth D. Dodds, *Marriage to a Difficult Man*, 22.

5 George M. Marsden, *Jonathan Edwards: A Life* (New Haven: Yale University Press, 2003), Locations 324–334.

6 Technically speaking, it was the First Great Awakening, but it will be referred to as simply the Great Awakening in this chapter for simplicity. The Second Great Awakening took place between 1800 and 1840 and had an equally profound impact on the nation, which was heading into the Civil War.

7 Marsden, *A Short Life.*

8 Ibid.

9 Dodds, 38.

10 Jonathan Claussen, MD, *Restoring the Power of Family* (Bloomington: Westbow, 2014), 129–130.

11 Mark W. Merrill, "Leadership Skills: A Father's Legacy," 2016. Accessed on February 21, 2016. http://www.allprodad.com/a-father's-legacy/.

Nine

THE AMERICAN DREAM

LIVING THE DREAM!

Born and raised in Mexico, Amado and his wife, Esperanza, first came to the United States on January 1, 1924. They stayed for a year visiting relatives, but at the urging of Esperanza, who wanted their baby to be born in Mexico, they returned home with all of two pesos to their name. Amado had worked on the railroad for much of his young life, but upon returning he was persuaded by his father-in-law that he could make more money by starting a business of his own. So starting out with one peso and a burro on loan from his father-in-law, Amado set out to the local supply store in town, where he proceeded to spend all that he had and then load it onto his borrowed burro. He purchased anything and everything that he could possibly sell to the ranchers and farmers who lived in the outlying areas. And it worked. It wasn't long before he was able to repay his father-in-law, purchase the borrowed burro, and begin sitting down to a large pile of money at the end of every day. He turned out to be a great salesman and would set out early each day with flour, bread, clothing, and whatever else he could find to sell, only to return home each night a man of success. In spite of his growing success, he still found himself discontented, longing for a home of his own and becoming increasingly uncertain as to whether or not that home would include his native Mexico.

It came about that on Easter Sunday of the following year, he was again doing quite well with his sales. So good, in fact, that he had gone out and returned three times already and was returning once more to reload. On this, his last load, however, all that was left to buy and to take back out were fireworks. So he bought all that he could possibly fit on that faithful burro of his, and he carefully began taking them out to be loaded. However, in the process, he slipped and fell, with much of the crate and its cargo exploding into his face and upper body. He was taken home that night by a couple of friends, covered with splinters, bloodied, and having lost his sight in both of his eyes. Within a few days, he had miraculously regained sight in his left eye (another story for another time, perhaps), but the right was no better. He needed a doctor, and the nearest one was a good distance away in Mexico City. Convinced that the journey would be worth their time, they set out on the long and very costly trip. When they finally arrived and he was examined by the doctor, it was determined that his vision would be impossible to restore without a transplant. The doctor offered him a glass eye, but between the cost of the trip and the doctor's visit, he could no longer afford it. Having lost everything once again, his father sent money and Amado took his family and returned to Texas in July 1926.

Amado worked at various jobs over the next several years, but he failed to settle into anything permanent, as he was still rather uncertain as to where they would call home.

True, the American people had been good to him thus far but still he wondered if he had made the right decision. As it turns out, his moment of decision finally came in 1939 with the start of WWII. In 1926, under President Hoover, the U.S. government had initiated an attempt to remove all illegal U.S. residents of Mexican descent. In the process, however, many *legal* non-citizens and *legal* U.S. citizens ended up being targets, as well. So, in 1939, with the United States pushing from their side, the president of Mexico, seeking to boost his own economy, saw an opportunity and began offering incentives of new land rights and all the equipment needed for clearing that land to anyone of Mexican descent who would choose to return to their mother country. Amado was a *legal* non-citizen and he did not need to leave; nevertheless, the offer was still very tempting. However, upon careful consideration and the advice of his father, Amado decided that Mexico could no longer be called home for him and his family. Living conditions had only continued to deteriorate there, and the risk of contracting illness and disease were more than he was willing to subject his young family to. With the uncertainty settled and the decision finally made, they began working and traveling as a family from Texas to Ohio, finding work in the fields wherever help was needed. Around the same time, his eldest son, Pete, was drafted into the U.S. Army, where he would serve his new country with great pride in the signal corps.

Upon Pete's return from the war, he encouraged his father to relocate and settle in Ohio, telling him that the road between Texas and Ohio had seen too many accidents and become too dangerous to keep traveling with the family. So in 1951 Amado and Esperanza saw their dream become reality as they purchased a home and some farmland in northwest Ohio. In addition to this, his family was now safe and his children—all eleven of them—could finish their schooling in one place. Inspired by this reality, and also by the fact that landowners were subject to the laws laid down by government officials on every level, Amado quickly recognized the value of having a voice in the decisions that were being made. Therefore, he decided to become a naturalized U.S. citizen in 1954. Indeed, the American people had been very good to them, and he was now very proud to officially become one of them.

Just two years later, in 1956, they bought a second home with some land, where my parents eventually settled and where I had the joy and privilege of growing up. My grandparents *lived* the American dream!

ORIGINS

Long before Washington, Jefferson, Adams, and the rest of the Founding Fathers were ever conceived, the American dream had already become a flourishing reality. From the time of its earliest settlers, America has always held the promise of unlimited possibilities for those who desired to start a new life and pursue their dreams to the fullest. Whether or not their dreams ever came into fruition did not really matter; what mattered was that people were free to *pursue* them. From the outcast to the farmer, the skilled tradesman to the businessman, America was no respecter of persons when it came to inspiring and releasing untapped potential within the human heart. Nevertheless, over the course of time, the ability to pursue one's dreams was slowly and progressively being stripped away and assaulted. More and more frequently, the people of the American colonies were being taxed unjustly, without fair and adequate representation, and they suffered repeated violations of their rights as British subjects under King George III. As a result, the people of the American colonies decided that a new nation was necessary to ensure their fair treatment. They had recognized and were now acknowledging that they had, in fact, been "endowed...with certain unalienable rights of Life, Liberty, and the pursuit of Happiness," which came from their Creator—and not King George. They told him as much in the Declaration of Independence.

In short, the American dream had come to embody the privilege and abilities that Americans had come to possess, independent of government. The fullness of these rights and privileges was spelled out within the Declaration, and they were soon to be forthcoming in our Constitution. Why were these considered to be independent of government? Because this government was never designed to create rights; it was established only to protect them. For *this* reason, our forefathers chose to break off from Britain, our mother country, in order to form a new and independent nation. Therefore, in essence, this nation and its government were established to protect and defend the American dream.

This too is a portion of our common ground—the freedom and ability to dream for ourselves, for our children, and for the communities in which we live. However, for many Americans, it is ground that needs to be reclaimed. The results taken from various polls between 2009 and 2015 tell us that approximately 50 percent of Americans reported still having, holding, and believing in the American dream.[1] Now, while it's encouraging that such a large portion of our nation still believes in the American dream, it also means that a very large segment (about 40 to 60 percent) has begun to disengage from reaching it. Why?

Dreaming is inherent to human nature. It is as much a part of our makeup and design as having two eyes, two ears, and a nose—maybe even more so. We dream about what we want to do someday, the type of person we want to marry, or perhaps about what we desire to provide for our families. So why has such a large portion of America begun to disconnect from the American dream? To be sure, the reasons are more vast and varied than we could ever cover with any clarity in this book. Yet, I believe there are a few overarching reasons that can and need to be explored, especially if you are one who has stopped or found yourself unable to dream.

THRIVE OR SURVIVE?

Several years ago I received a book for Christmas from my boss entitled *The Dream Manager* by Matthew Kelly. In typical employee fashion, I was insulted first and foremost by the fact that my Christmas present was a book instead of a cash bonus, and second I was irritated by its title. As I saw it, I had been given a book intended to help me become my boss's dream of a perfect manager within the company. So, like any good employee, I shelved it. Now, whether it was boredom or curiosity that eventually inspired me to take the book down from the shelf, I really don't recall, but when I finally did, I was more than pleasantly surprised. Instead of a book that would help me become my boss's ideal manager, I discovered that my boss was actually interested in what my dreams were. Shocking, right?

Kelly took me through the spellbinding story of a company that decided to invest in the dreams of its employees. After five years of investing in their employees' dreams, home ownership had tripled among employees, employee consumer debt had been reduced by 40 percent, turnover within the company had dropped from over 400 percent down to 12 percent, the company's gross revenue had *tripled*, and they were now employing nearly *twice* as many employees! So, what was the bottom line? Not only is dreaming a natural part of our design as human beings, but when dreams are properly encouraged and cared for, they will change your life and the lives of those around you!

Yet, while relaying the importance of dreams and the necessity to pursue them throughout a lifetime, the author also began to point out some of the things that keep people from dreaming. One of them is *survival mode*. When the bills begin stacking up, the creditors start calling, you see that you need a new muffler on the car, and you don't have the time to spend with your children that you desire (much less accomplish all that needs to be done for work), you have entered survival mode! Survival mode takes place when all your time and energy is focused on accomplishing the bare essentials needed in order to survive. There is no time for anything else. When we find ourselves stuck here, far too often we also stop dreaming.

> It is easy to get so caught up in surviving that we stop dreaming. When we stop dreaming, we slowly begin to disengage from our work, from our relationships, and from life itself![2]

Little by little, passion and energy begins to disappear from our lives. But while survival is important, it means little or nothing if we stop dreaming. (Some of you need to reread that last sentence and let it sink in for a moment.)

IMPOSSIBILITIES

The dream that *looks* impossible often is. Therefore, what is needed is a change in perspective. In fact, I believe that many of the 50 percent of Americans who say they no longer believe in the American dream have not actually stopped dreaming. They have merely stopped *believing* that their dreams are *possible*. So again, we need to ask—why?

To answer this one, I turn to my father. Whether he remembers it or not, I have often heard him say, "If you hang with [Poop], you're going to smell like it!" We pick up and carry the *aroma* of the things or people with whom we spend the most time. I believe that many of us have decided to give up on our dreams because we have been hanging out with or listening to individuals who reinforce the notion that achieving dreams is impossible and not worth chasing after. The message can come from friends, family members, the government, and oftentimes from so-called experts. Yet when we are surrounded by those who are willing to believe the impossible with us, believing and pursuing our dreams becomes much more attainable.

"One of the primary responsibilities of all relationships is to help each other fulfill our dreams!"[3] I will even go so far as to say that if your friends, family members, or government do not or cannot encourage you to pursue your dreams, you have got some potentially serious dysfunction in your relationships. Supporting and encouraging each other in pursuing our dreams is a portion of what every man, woman, and child is called to do and to be on the earth. We are called to be *dream managers* for those with whom we are in relationship.

Most things that are now a reality were once believed by many to be impossible. Yet all it took was one person who dared to believe and put faith in the fact that the impossible was indeed possible. However, believing alone is not enough. Faith is also needed. And faith requires action, which is usually spelled *R-I-S-K*. Ben Franklin believed that electricity could be harnessed and utilized, but until he took the risk of flying his kite during a thunderstorm to prove it, his belief got him nowhere. Pursuing our dreams will always require a certain amount of risk or investment. It is always possible to pursue dreams on our own, and nobody holds us back from doing so. We alone are responsible for our unfulfilled dreams. But when others come alongside of us and place themselves in submission to our dreams (the prefix *sub* literally means "under"—true submission is placing yourself under someone else's *mission* in life and pushing up!), everyone benefits.

SUBSTITUTES

Finally, it is important to recognize that one of the byproducts of living in survival mode is the quick fix. While it is true that being in survival mode often puts a stop to dreaming, it does not necessarily stop us from *wanting* to dream. Typically, we still desire to dream, but we lack the time or the energy to do it, much less pursue it. So we substitute.

Substitutes for pursuing the American dream can range from things such as power, fame, and fortune—to food, unhealthy relationships, toys, and much, much more. Often these are things that can no doubt give us pleasure for a time and could even be a part of our dreams, but in and of themselves they can never truly satisfy. Many a person has accumulated wealth, power, and fame, only to realize that in the end they had missed their true calling and purpose for existing, and knowing full well that it was now too late. The momentary gratification of the flesh can bring pleasure, but it can never satisfy.

Perhaps James Truslow Adams said it best when he first began defining and describing the wonder of the American dream in his 1931 book, *The Epic of America*. He stated:

> The American Dream is that dream of a land in which life should be better and richer and fuller for everyone, with opportunity for each according to ability or achievement. It is a difficult dream for the European upper classes to interpret adequately, and too many of us ourselves have grown weary and mistrustful of it. It is not a dream of motor cars and high wages merely, but a dream [whereby] each man and each woman shall be able to attain to the fullest stature of which they are innately capable, and be recognized by others for what they are, regardless of the fortuitous circumstances of birth or position.[4]

In other words, the American dream is pursuing our heart's desires beyond mere momentary pleasure to something that calls from deep within, giving us a purpose to work toward in life, and offering long-term satisfaction once it is accomplished.

> The American dream is that foundational building block of American society that cannot be improved upon; it is essential to our survival as a free nation.

So what are your hopes, dreams, and desires? For my grandfather it was simple: to live in a place of financial freedom and provide a place whereby he and his family could live, grow, and prosper, to secure a place where each successive generation had the opportunity to do the same or better than he did. What is the American dream for you? Are you pursuing it? Or have you simply become complacent with the status quo? Have you become so caught up in surviving that you've stopped dreaming or have settled for cheap substitutes? Have you believed the lies told by those around you who say that your dream is impossible to pursue, and that your lack of success is someone else's fault? What other excuse might you have for not pursuing your God-given calling in life, which many identify as the American dream?

We stand together upon this common ground of dreaming, pursuing, and realizing the American dream. We have no good excuse for not pursuing it. Repeatedly going after your dreams and failing is better than getting to the end of your life and realizing that you have never pursued them at all. We are called to pursue our dreams, and we are called to submit to one another in an effort to help each other do so. It requires time, patience, and work, but it is well worth the effort. As the individual achieves his or her dreams, all those around them benefit as well. Jobs are *not* created by government. They are created when Americans are free and encouraged to pursue their dreams. As individuals achieve their dreams, others become employed in work that provides the necessities required for *them* to pursue *their* dreams, and so forth.

Thus, if the American dream truly is a portion of what we are called to pursue regardless of social status, religion, ethnic background, or gender—then so too is *work*.

RECOMMENDED READING

Matthew Kelly, *The Dream Manager*, 2007.

—Great book, and most of it reads just like a good story. If you are stuck in the area of dreaming or being unable to dream, this may be a good place to start!

Notes

1 John Zogby. Zogby International, January 30, 2009. Accessed on July 6, 2010. http://www.zogby.com/news/ReadNews.cfm?ID=1674; Ciaran O'Connor and Laura Czaja, "The Atlantic/Aspen Institute Survey: Majority of Americans Express Optimism About Own Lives, Yet Believe American Dream Is Suffering," July 1, 2015. Accessed on February 28, 2016. http://www.prnewswire.com/news-releases/new-the-atlanticaspen-institute-survey-majority-of-americans-express-optimism-about-own-lives-yet-believe-american-dream-is-suffering-300107748.html; Camille Noe Pagan, "Do Americans still believe in the American Dream?" December 10, 2013. Accessed February 28, 2016. htttp://theweek.com/articles/454865/americans-still-believe-american-dream.

2 Matthew Kelly, *The Dream Manager* (New York: Hyperion, 2007).

3 Ibid.

4 James Truslow Adams, *The Epic of America* (Boston: Little, Brown, and Company, 2931), 214–215.

Ten

THE NECESSITY OF WORK

The American dream is impossible without hard work. Millions of Americans go to work each day with the hope of pursuing their dreams either directly (in what they do) or indirectly (i.e., by making money to use to pursue their dreams). And while it is hardly necessary (or even desirable, in many cases) to consider the multitude of merits, pitfalls, and values associated with work, there are a few concepts that bear mentioning and are most profitable when understood and applied. To that end, I wish to share with you an adaptation of one of my favorite childhood stories. Because sometimes concepts are better illustrated than taught, with a topic like *work* perhaps it is best to begin with a child's perspective.

THE TREE

Once upon a time, in the middle of a beautiful forest, there lived a tree. And the tree loved the affections of the people who lived in the nearby village. For, you see, it was the responsibility and appointed task of each tree in the forest to serve the people of that village by giving of their fruit, providing shade, and assisting them in whatever way they possibly could. And their reward was simply this—the undying affections and appreciation of the people.

Every day the children would come and play underneath the tree. And when they grew tired they would sit down at its base and eat its fruit in the shade. The other trees in the forest also liked and even desired the affections of the children, but they would seldom tolerate their games and rough play; nor did they feel they could afford to give them any of their fruit, though most of them were heavy-laden with it. Because this tree gave so freely, the children loved it very much, and the tree was happy. But as time went by and the children grew older, the tree was often left alone.

But as the tree soon discovered, the children could not stay away. For they had seen and experienced for themselves the love and the selflessness of the tree over and over as they were growing up.

Time and again the children would return, and the tree would give everything it had to fill their needs. When the tree offered for one of the children to take all its fruit, the other trees shuddered at the very thought of losing all their fruit at once. They seemed to straighten all the taller when they heard this, so that the children wouldn't get the same crazy idea of stripping them of all their fruit.

Another child returned in need of lumber and upon hearing this, the other trees trembled and began to shake. Several of them even began dropping off as many of their dead branches as they could, hoping that the boy would use them instead. After all, better for all of them to give a little than for any one of them to lose all their beautiful branches. However, many of these dead branches were not very big, nor even suitable for building. But the tree gave all of its best and strongest branches.

At long last, the tree had given everything possible, including its great and powerful trunk in service to the children and the people of the village. And the tree was happy for a while. But soon it became very sad and disheartened. For why would any of the children now return? It had nothing left to give.

But even that did not stop the children. Although they were now getting old and gray, the tree soon found it was more popular than ever. For an old stump is a wonderful place to sit, rest, and release all the cares and worries of the world.

Now then, years later, as the mayor of the village was walking through the forest, he began to notice that many of the trees still had rotting fruit on their branches, which also covered the ground beneath them. (After all, since they were afraid to give out too much of their fruit, many gave out very little in the end.) And upon seeing all the dead and decaying branches, which they had also shaken to the ground while trying to avoid becoming a house, the mayor decided that it was finally time. For you see, when the mayor was still very young, he too would go and play in his favorite tree, the only one that now lay as a rotting stump. And when he was done playing, he would take of the tree's fruit, eat it on the way home, and then spit the seeds into an empty barrel on his porch. This barrel now sat in his basement filled to the brim with the seeds he had taken from his favorite tree. He had seen an entire generation of villagers served by this forest. But for all the fruit and lumber that had been given to help the villagers, nothing compared to the service given by this tree. In fact, throughout the village this tree had become the most praiseworthy and the most talked about tree in the entire forest.

So, gathering some help from the other villagers, the mayor began to construct a beautiful garden in the town square, complete with many of the world's most exotic and expensive plants and flowers. In the center of the garden, the mayor planted a few of the best seeds that he had taken from the barrel, in memory of this most beloved of trees. Upon finishing the garden, he and the villagers stood back, admired their work, and inwardly stirred with the anticipation of watching this young tree grow. They proceeded to the forest, where they cut down the remainder of the trees, threw their scraps on a large pile, and burnt them. And taking what was left of the mayor's barrel, they began to reseed the entire forest. (Story inspired by the book *The Giving Tree*[1])

THE FRUITS OF LABOR...

First of all, if there is something that we desire, we will only receive it to the fullest extent by *giving* our all, much like this tree did. There is a direct correlation between work and reward. True, the illusory shortcut will always be there (as with anything that is worth having in life), but nothing short of giving our best effort will ever be a worthy substitute. Though we do not often see it modeled in our current work culture, it needs to be recognized and acknowledged that *how* we accomplish a job is often just as important as accomplishing a job itself, and therefore, it should also affect the reward. This is an area of common ground for employers and employees alike.

If we are *employees*, this means that we are called upon to do our jobs as though *we* are the business owner. Think about that for a moment. If we suddenly became the owner of the business where we are currently employed, would we do our work any differently than we currently do? Would we take the shortcut to cleaning "that machine" so that we get our work done faster, or would we do it properly so as to prolong the life of "that machine" and prevent us from paying the extra cost of repair or replacement? Would we aim to barely make our quota of minimum work each day, or would we aim to do as much as we possibly could, above and beyond our quota, so that *we* could earn more and allow *our* business to thrive and grow? Would we treat our customers with contempt (or whatever emotions we felt that day), or would we seek to treat each customer as a king or queen, regardless of our mood (or how we felt), knowing that the loss of even a single customer could drastically affect *our* company's profit? If we would want our company to thrive and maximize our own profits as a hypothetical owner, then we should give no less as employees. When we are hired for any job, we agree to perform certain duties for a specified wage. Regardless of the job, there is an expectation that we will do our job to the best of our ability.

If, as the hypothetical owner, we would also desire or expect a certain level of work and conduct from our employees, then this is what we owe to our present employers, regardless of what we think of them or how we feel we have been treated by them. If we have grievances, then we basically have three honorable choices: 1) address the grievances with our employers through the proper channels until they are resolved; 2) not address things and keep our mouths shut; or 3) find a new job. If we choose not to address our grievances, it's our own fault. And if this is our choice, then we need to be ready to suck it up, keep our mouths shut so as not to infect the other employees, and continue to perform our work to the best of our abilities. We cannot expect our employers to fix what is broken if we are not willing to tell them about it, and we cannot expect to be rewarded with raises, promotions, and bonuses, if we are not willing to give them our all.

Business owners and *employers*, if we desire our employees to work in this manner, then we need to commit ourselves to encouraging a work environment in which open communication is safe and encouraged, and we need to make our expectations clear. We need to equip our employees properly so that they can effectively and efficiently do what we desire them to do—and then be ready to reward those who do. Our employees affect our bottom line. When we invest in order to make a quality product, customers are better satisfied, and we see a higher profit margin. Yes, we need to continue investing in our product, but when we put a similar effort into investing in our people, we will reap the same reward and more.

Now, perhaps I have just overstated the obvious by putting things into such an ideal picture. Yet this "reality of the ideal" is exactly what we need to be reminded of, in spite of the "reality" in which we live or how we may perceive our situation to be. Sometimes we have no clue how to fix things or what to strive for until we are faced with the "plumb line" of the ideal.

REAPING AND SOWING...

Second, like the law of gravity, the law of sowing and reaping is a very real but yet unseen force in the world. For example, if we sow apple seeds, we will reap apple trees and apples. If we put time and effort into caring for those seeds, we will get really good trees that produce really good apples. America used to be known for putting out really "good apples." Yet, as a nation, many business owners and workers have gotten so tied up in their own *personal* bottom lines that quality has greatly suffered across the board, and now "buying American" no longer means what it used to mean.

When they were first established, labor unions in America were designed to protect the rights of the common worker, prevent abuse, and help keep employers accountable for their actions. Yet through the years, some of these unions have become just as responsible as the business owners themselves for the rising prices and steady decline in the workmanship of American-made products. At one time, business owners (although not all of them) were known and expected to "bully" their workers (and some still do) in order to increase their profits regardless of the "costs" to the employee. Ironically enough, we now find that many (though not all) labor unions have become the "bullies" to affect the personal profit margins of union leaders and employees regardless of the cost to the employers or the customers. In many cases, one might say that these business owners are merely reaping what they have sown. Regardless, the result is that both "bullies" find themselves in a stalemate, putting out an inferior product at a ridiculous cost, all the while shouting to the American people, "Buy American—it's a matter of pride!" Well, if pride had at all been taken in the quality of workmanship they were truly giving to the free market, they would not need to shout.

A good quality product sells itself. It always has, and it always will! If a company and its workers strive to this end, there will be no limit to the number of Americans as well as people from around the world who will beat a path to their door. For *this* reason we should take pride in the label, "Made in America"—quality. However, if a company and its workers give us inferior products for the same price or greater than something that is better made, why should they be rewarded with our business, much less any pride in their work?! And if a company can no longer survive because it cannot put out a good product at a reasonable cost, then it should be allowed to die and reap what it has sown. Good workers will always find other jobs or start their own businesses to fill the gap. *America owes a job to no one. It is the land of "opportunity"—not the land of "you owe me."* There is no such thing as a guaranteed job. We have the *opportunity* to find employment or to start a business of our own. And whether employer or employee, make no mistake about it, each assumes a certain amount of risk. A businessperson risks his fortunes and together with his employees they both risk (literally put their faith in) the survival of the company. If they do well, there is reward for both, but if not, there is the opportunity for one or both to start over. Sometimes ideas fail, and we just need to get over it and start again.

Like the giving tree, when we "sow" by giving the best of all we have to give, we will undoubtedly be rewarded for our labors. We should "buy American" when and if we can take pride in the quality of the products coming out of American companies, as well as the ability and ingenuity of that company (and its workers) to bring forth the product at an affordable price. Taking pride in a company just because it is American is as foolish as saying that I should take pride in the fact that Charles Manson was born and raised in America. *Quality matters!* And when we sow a quality product through a quality effort, we will reap a quality reward! If we do not, then, like the trees in our story...we should get "fired."

I'M ONLY A STUMP!

Finally, when we focus on our lack, we shall always find it. Even the tree came to a point that it could not see what (if anything) it had left to offer. Why? Because it was focusing on itself.

We can all come to the point in life, whether through circumstances of our own making or not, where all we can see is our loss, our lack, and/or our need. We question, what more could we possibly have to offer people? These can be very difficult and even trying times, and we often view them as the end of our days. Yet as difficult as these times can be, I want to encourage you to take the focus off of yourself for a moment. When you do that, you will find two things: One, there are *always* people worse off than you are. And two, there is *always* something we can do to further contribute to society. *There are no good reasons, no excuses, for a person not to work.*

Between the variety of jobs, fair labor laws, and technological advances for persons with disabilities, there are absolutely no excuses left. Am I calling you lazy? No, that is not for me to judge. But let me ask *you*...are you being lazy? Only complete honesty can reveal the answer. But whether you are lazy, depressed, angry, or disabled, the problem in the end always comes back to your focus...you.

Regardless of who you are or what your circumstances may be, I encourage you to begin by asking for God's help in changing your focus. *We are all born with purpose, and our circumstances do not change that fact.* We need to look beyond the mirror and realize that even a stump has purpose!

Without hard work and risk, it is guaranteed that the American dream will never come into fruition…fulfillment will be temporary at best.

THE BIG PICTURE…

There is much talk about the state of our economy in America right now, and with good reason. The topic is batted around like a political hot potato in the media, and to be certain there are numerous reasons for the present state of our economy, many of which point to the failure of our representatives in the federal government. *But putting politics and all else aside for the moment, we have the opportunity to directly affect the state of our economy each and every day through good, old-fashioned hard work.*

When we work to the best of our ability, we put out a good product. And when we put out a good product, we increase demand for that product. When demand is increased, it necessitates the buying of more goods and raw materials, and the hiring of more people to help make the product that we are putting out. And when we take the focus off of ourselves, we begin looking for jobs again, or taking steps toward becoming our own boss, which means fewer people on public assistance, more people contributing to the general welfare of the country, and an economy that begins to climb out from the gutter.

We have the power and ability to directly affect and impact the American economy by what we do each day. *This* is our common lot, and a foundational component of godly capitalism. However, if we are going to commit to doing our part to the best of our ability, then we do need to ask, "What role and responsibility *does* our government play in all of this?"

And, "What role *should* it play?" Before we can properly consider this, we first need to take a closer look at another foundational component of the American economy. With the vast majority of our politicians and the popular media pushing us toward socialism at the present time, we need now more than ever to reconsider the true *heart* of capitalism.

RECOMMENDED READING:

Shel Silverstein, *The Giving Tree*, 1964.

—Okay, yes, it's a children's book. But quite honestly, his original rendition is very good and presents a profound truth, with childlike simplicity. Plus, his book contains cool illustrations. If nothing else, pick it up to read to your kids or grandkids.

Notes

1 Shel Silverstein, *The Giving Tree* (New York: Harper-Collins, 1964).

Eleven

PURSUING THE HEART
OF CAPITALISM

OVERPRICED VACUUM CLEANERS

Shortly after we were married, my wife and I responded to a newspaper ad that promised two large bottles of Pepsi just for calling. We were young, naïve, and liked Pepsi, so I called. The lady who answered was very nice. She politely asked for my name and phone number, and then whether or not we liked Pepsi, for I soon found out she was willing to give us another brand of soda if we did not. Nevertheless, I assured her that we did, indeed, like Pepsi. She then proceeded to tell me that she would be sending someone out who would actually *bring* the Pepsi to us in return for "just a moment of our time" so that they could show us a new product. We really liked Pepsi, and it was free. So, I gave her our address (figuring that we could endure *any* salesman for a little while), and continued setting up a time for this nice man to bring us our Pepsi and show us this new product.

The next evening, there came a knock at the apartment door right on schedule, and I opened it to find a nicely dressed man carrying two large cases. Assuming that our Pepsi must be in one of those cases, I invited him in. Before we could think twice about when we would receive the much-sought-after *free* Pepsi, this nicely dressed man pulled out a "state of the art" vacuum cleaner from the very depths of his cases. It was bright and shiny, and was made with "space-age technology," such as the eyes of few mortal men had ever seen before. An hour later, after seeing various types of dirt and black soot removed from our carpet and hearing yet another story about this vacuum cleaner and how its ancestral line could be traced back to "nuclear submarines," you guessed it—we bit! For just one thousand dollars we bought ourselves the latest and greatest in vacuum technology that would "last a lifetime" and beyond. Our children and their children would call us *blessed*, as this family heirloom would be passed from one generation to the next!

Well, as I was helping this nice man (who by now was sweating profusely from his sweeper demonstration) down to his car in order to retrieve our new "heirloom" from his trunk, I finally remembered why we had called him in the first place…the free Pepsi! So, as I triumphantly received my new vacuum cleaner, "the last one in stock" from the trunk of his car, I asked if he had also brought our Pepsi. He paused and looked at me for a moment, as though I had suddenly grown a third nostril, before a look of realization finally came across his face and he said, "Oh yeah!" He reached into his trunk one more time to pull out a bag from the grocery store right down the street, which contained our two bottles of Pepsi.

I thanked him for his time, picked up my packages once again, and proudly strutted back toward our apartment to show my lovely bride the spoils of victory; I had conquered! However, somewhere between the trunk of his car and the door to our fourth-floor apartment, it suddenly dawned on me just how much we had paid for those two bottles of Pepsi that I now carried.

THE VALUE OF HISTORY

My wife and I estimate that we have gone through at least six vacuum cleaners since we first purchased our "family heirloom" (which, by the way, has recently gone to the curb). My father often warned me when I was growing up not to believe everything I see or hear, especially as it relates to salesmen. Had I *remembered* and listened to his advice, I might have seen the vacuum cleaner salesman's pitch coming. However, mistakes happen, and all things considered, ours was relatively small. Still, it is a lesson that, if not learned early on in life, has the potential of costing us much more than just money.

When someone shows up at your door with a product that you are completely unfamiliar with, even the most astute buyer is at a disadvantage. The same applies when you are presented with *new* concepts, ideas, and ways of doing things. The person might have a great *product* to sell you, which may be more than worth your time and money, but yet at other times it may turn out to be nothing more than an overpriced vacuum cleaner. So, what do you do when you find yourself at such a disadvantage, with no advice or experience to lean upon?

Caveat emptor, quia ignorare non debuit quod jus alienum emit. Translated, this phrase means "let the purchaser beware, for he ought not to be ignorant of the nature of the property that he is buying from another party."[1] Thus, if you find yourself ignorant of a product, concept, or idea, cure that ignorance by researching its *history* before making a decision. Herein lies the value of history! It is so much more than the class we may have disliked growing up, and even then we must acknowledge that our view of studying history is greatly influenced by the manner in which it is taught. Nevertheless, to the one who takes the time to consider it, history holds immeasurable worth. Whether measured in physical, spiritual, or emotional wealth and well-being, the value of history is equal to, or even greater than, the cost of the potential setbacks and utter failures that knowing and applying it would have otherwise caused us to avoid. In other words, if I have previously lost ten dollars through foolish mistakes but avoid losing a thousand dollars by knowing and applying that history, then history itself has a *real* value.

Consider the Israelites. God had performed many miraculous signs and wonders in the process of delivering them from slavery. Even before they left Egypt, Moses admonished them not to forget what God had done, what they had seen with their own eyes and knew to be true from experience: that God was faithful! Yet before they could even make it to the Promised Land, an entire generation had yielded themselves to the persuasive words of a few who, in essence, "sold" them the idea that "God is *not* faithful" and that "we are better off on our own!" As a result of the cunning salesmanship of those who thought they knew better than God, an entire generation perished in the desert. Fortunately, however, most of *their* children (along with Joshua and Caleb from the previous generation) remembered God's promise and His faithfulness, and after forty years they were finally able to enter into the Promised Land and possess it. Tragically, their parents had bought themselves an "overpriced vacuum cleaner"—at the cost of their very lives. *Truly, when we forget our history, the consequences can be devastating.*

So then, what does all of this have to do with capitalism? Regardless of whom you ask and what their political persuasion may be, many people will tell you that the present state of capitalism in America (or rather, how it is presently functioning) is "broken." Their reasoning and proposed solutions will be vast and varied, but many would agree that this is true and a very real problem affecting our national economy. To that end, if our politicians and leaders would be willing to study the country's history, beyond the motive of justifying their own positions, they would find that, indeed, *remembering* might be one of the greatest keys to fixing it.

CAPITALISM 101

Before properly engaging in a discussion about capitalism, we need to be sure we have the same thing in mind, so let's start by defining it. *Capitalism* is an *economic system* (a way in which a nation chooses to manage and organize its production, distribution, and consumption of goods and services) based upon *private ownership* (the ability to own and accumulate things as individuals) and *entrepreneurship* (the choice to start businesses, create products, or provide services). The simple definition is the graphic on the next page.

Capitalism allows me as an individual to be the one to take the risk and start the business, or to simply be someone who works for the business owner. Either way I am free to accumulate wealth, save it, spend it, give it away to whomever I choose, or do nothing with it at all.

Capitalism works based on supply and demand. The more competition there is to make or provide any given product or

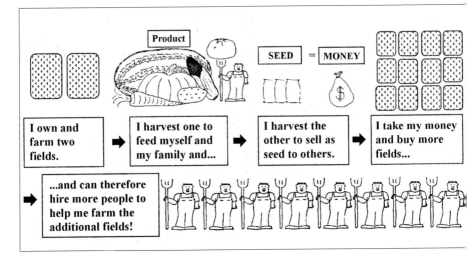

service, the better deals consumers will receive from those businesses making that product or providing those services. For example, let's say I make and sell a doghouse, of which there are very few, therefore the supply for my doghouse is down, and the demand for my doghouse goes up (because there are so few doghouses available and people want them), allowing me to sell my doghouses at a higher price. However, if another person comes along and begins making a similar doghouse, the supply of that doghouse (which we are now both making) is greater, and there are more doghouses to sell. As a result, I will need to lower my prices in order to compete with the other business owner(s), and the consumers (those who desire to buy our doghouses) end up getting much better deals. This, in a nutshell, is capitalism.

Now, while we are at it, let us consider another term that is pertinent to our discussion. Let us now define socialism. *Socialism* is an economic system based upon *state ownership* (the idea that the government owns everything, and individuals own very little, if anything) and *control* (the government controls basically everything, from food distribution, to schools, health care, all television programs and other forms of media, and so on) of all production, distribution, and consumption of goods and services. According to *Merriam-Webster*, *socialism* is "the transitional stage *between capitalism and communism and is distinguished by unequal distribution of goods and pay according to work done.*"[2] The simple definition of socialism looks more like this:

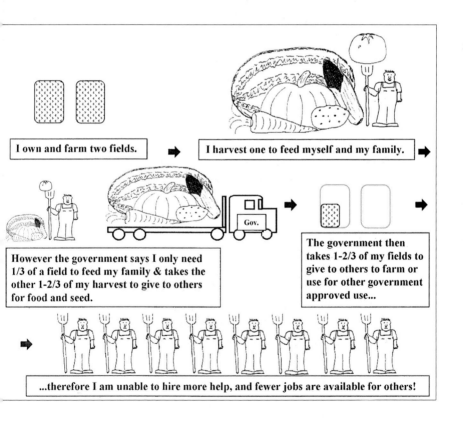

I own and farm two fields.

I harvest one to feed myself and my family.

However the government says I only need 1/3 of a field to feed my family & takes the other 1-2/3 of my harvest to give to others for food and seed.

The government then takes 1-2/3 of my fields to give to others to farm or use for other government approved use...

...therefore I am unable to hire more help, and fewer jobs are available for others!

With this model, I get to keep 1/6, or around 16 percent, of my original property, which belongs to me for as long as the government finds it convenient to allow me to "have" it. Socialism, therefore, does not allow for businesses to be owned by individuals without a strong degree of governmental control (regulations) over its production, distribution, and profits. Products are made, and prices for those products are determined based upon what the government decides is needed and what prices are considered fair.

The accumulation of wealth (while possible in theory) is discouraged in socialism, as it is looked upon as unfair for any individual to have more than his fellow man. So, wealth *can* be accumulated in a socialistic society, but it *must* be redistributed through heavy taxation to give to others who are not capable or willing to produce their own.

There is also no need to give to others because what you give will be determined by the government (not you) as it redistributes your earnings, which you surrender to them in the form of mandatory taxes as high as 60 to 70 percent (or more!) of your entire paycheck.

Price controls are set by the government, and the effect is that there are no deals to be had by the consumer because there is no competition. With no competition, there are seldom (if ever) any new or improved products (or advances in health care) because there is no motivation for most people to create, since they are no longer able to reap the reward of accumulating wealth or personal property. *Sooner or later, every facet of life becomes controlled and regulated by the governing authorities.* And this, in a nutshell, is socialism.

NOW, SO WHAT, AND WHO CARES?

How, then, does one even begin to fix capitalism? The same way you fix any other mechanism or machine when it is broken—you begin by asking lots of questions. For example, we might ask, how was it supposed to work? How did it work in peak performance? What was it composed of? How was it put together? What broke it to begin with? And can we add safeguards to keep it from breaking again? If we can remember or research its history, the answers to all of these questions and the solutions (or ways of fixing it) are within our grasp. We can fix a *thing* or even replace it with something *similar* (of like kind) by knowing its history. For example, if we have a flat tire and the jack is broken, we replace it with a new jack of a similar type that will raise the car high enough to repair the tire. Conversely, we would not attempt to raise the car off of the ground by using a pipe bomb. Would it raise the car off of the ground? Yes, but it would also do irreparable damage and the car would be ruined. No, we need to raise the car off of the ground by either repairing the original jack or buying a new one. It may or may not look a little different, but it will function in the same manner and it might even work better than the original. So, too, with capitalism!

There is a very small but very loud and persuasive group of individuals (many of them holding public office) who are trying to convince the American public that they need an "overpriced vacuum cleaner." Their goal is to attempt to "fix" capitalism with a "pipe bomb" called socialism. And, in all honesty, they are great salesmen. But then again, those who have traditionally tried to sell socialism typically are.

In 1938 Austria transferred power to Nazi Germany (the German National Socialist Party) without a single shot being fired. Instead, power was granted to Adolf Hitler by a vote of support over 98 percent.[3] Was the vote rigged? Possibly, but that too is a part of the salesmanship. Even if nobody wants it, make it look like everybody does! In truth it's likely that many truly wanted German control as Austria was stuck in the middle of an economic depression and times were tough. Could they get any worse under Hitler?

A woman who actually lived through that change had this to say:

> Before Hitler, we had very good medical care. Many American doctors trained at the University of Vienna. After Hitler, health care was socialized, free for everyone. Doctors were salaried by the government. The problem was, since it was free, people were going to the doctors for everything. When the good doctor arrived at his office at 8 a.m., forty people were already waiting, and, at the same time, the hospitals were full. If you needed elective surgery, you had to wait a year or two for your turn. There was no money for research as it was poured into socialized medicine. Research at the medical schools literally stopped, so the best doctors left Austria and emigrated to other countries. As for health care, our tax rates went up to 80 percent of our income.
>
> We were told how to shop and what to buy. Free enterprise was essentially abolished.
>
> Totalitarianism didn't come quickly; it took five years, from 1938 until 1943, to realize full dictatorship in Austria. Had it happened overnight, my countrymen would have fought to the last breath. Instead,

we had creeping gradualism. The whole idea sounds almost unbelievable, that the state, little by little, eroded our freedom.[4]

Yes, capitalism in its present state may be "broken," but socialism is not the answer.

GOD'S IDEA

In truth, I do not have all of the answers for these questions, yet I can tell you this: If we are to fix whatever may be broken with capitalism in this nation, we must study history carefully and acknowledge that capitalism was God's idea first. Consider what God said to Moses in Deuteronomy 8:18 (NASB):

> *But you shall remember the Lord your God, for it is He who is giving you power to make wealth, that He may confirm His covenant which He swore to your fathers, as it is this day.*

God gives the power, the gift of *ability*, to make wealth. Regardless of what we may do with that gift, it is given freely and it is ours to do with as we please. Some will use it for the good purpose for which it was intended, and others will not. And to what covenant was God referring? The one made with Abraham when He promised him that He would give the land of Canaan to Abraham and his descendants.

> God was positioning Abraham and his descendants so their economic system would be founded on the ownership of land—a foundation necessary for capitalism to flourish.[5]

Harold Eberle is one of my favorite authors, and he has published an enlightening book entitled *Compassionate Capitalism*. In it Harold does a masterful job of establishing that capitalism was, indeed, God's idea. He further demonstrates a thorough knowledge and summary of the history of capitalism. Consider this:

> The principles of capitalism developed as God worked among the Hebrew people in the Old Testament times…. However, it is important to note that the capitalism seen in the Bible is not the same as that which we have today. Their form of capitalism went hand in hand with social values, including care for the elderly, orphans, and widows. God also instilled certain restrictions on capitalism to protect His people from abuses and oppression.[6]

I personally believe that there are more Americans who see the value of maintaining a certain degree of social care and assistance as a nation than there are true socialists. In fact, social programs are not bad if, in fact, they promote and encourage liberty and freedom. But when they cease doing so and begin creating an *entitlement mentality* and a *dependency* upon the programs, then it is time to reexamine the programs so that they can be reworked or, if necessary, removed. Eberle went on to write:

> On the negative side, capitalism which is separated from godly values ignores the needs of those unable to care for themselves, such as the disabled, orphans, widows, elderly, and mentally ill. Over the course of many years, it can create a huge disparity between the rich and the poor. A capitalistic economy

can also open the door for greed, leading to the acceleration of the pace at which society moves, eventually entrapping people in a rat race of commercialism and materialism. Finally, unlimited capitalism allows for the unscrupulous person to deplete our resources and destroy the environment.

Strict capitalists would rather not discuss these negatives, but at the other extreme are socialists who focus on these negatives so much that they end up totally rejecting the concept of capitalism as a viable economic system.

What is the proper approach? We must nurture a capitalistic economy but govern it with wisdom. We need to deal with the flaws and abuses of capitalism without squelching initiative, creativity, entrepreneurship, and industrialism. People must be allowed the right to life, liberty, and the pursuit of happiness. However, society as a whole must apply godly values and carry the responsibility to meet the needs of the helpless.[7]

In my opinion, Eberle sets the standard and does an outstanding job in accurately conveying the true heart and nature of capitalism at its best.

A capitalistic society was God's idea first. It need not be oppressive, uncaring, or exclusive. Either we find and nurture the true heart of capitalism, or we shall most assuredly cease to exist as a free nation.

As I stated earlier, I do not have all the answers for fixing capitalism, but Eberle's book is a great place to start. It's short, simple, easy enough to read, and straight to the point; I highly recommend it. And when you are finished, send a copy to your state and federal representatives, as well. In light of the fact that some have been found who do not even read (much less understand) the legislation that they pass, this is a good book for them; it's short enough that even a U.S. Congressman or Senator could read it and enjoy.

RECOMMENDED READING

Harold R. Eberle, *Compassionate Capitalism: A Judeo-Christian Value*, 2010.

—What more can I say? Good stuff; check it out!

Notes

1 Elizabeth Knowles, *The Oxford Dictionary of Phrase and Fable*, "buyer," 2006. Accessed on January 12, 2012. http://www.encyclopedia.com.

2 *Merriam-Webster*, "socialism," 2010. Accessed on August 30, 2010. http://www.merriam-webster.com/dictionary/socialism.

3 History.com Staff, History.com, Hitler announces an Anschluss with Austria, 2009, Accessed on September 28, 2016, http://www.history.com/this-day-in-history/hitler-announces-an-anschluss-with-austria

4 Kitty Werthmann, ResistNet.com, December 16, 2009. Accessed on September 1, 2010. http://www.resistnet.com/profiles/blogs/1938-austria-land-of-the; Kitty Werthmann, Camp America speech, October 6, 2010. Accessed on March 14, 2012. http://www.youtube.com/watch?v=Mr9777ugCiM.

5 Eberle, Harold R., *Compassionate Capitalism, A Judeo-Christian Value*. Yakima: Worldcast Publishing, 2010. pp. 1-2, 10.

6 Ibid.

7 Ibid.

~ Twelve ~

IMPROVING UPON EQUALITY

If we are to find our common ground in this nation, we must we have a firm understanding of the true nature of *equality*. Therefore, since the greatest misuse and corruption of this concept appear to be in relation to money, let us seek to understand it in relation to the two most relevant sub-groups that exist in this nation: the *rich* and the *poor*.

PROBING OUR PARADIGM

Whom would you trust more: a man who grew up poor in a small farming town, or a man worth billions of dollars? Which one is more likely to be generous? Which one knows better the value of hard work? Which one is more mechanically inclined? Which one knows more about equality? Have you got your answers? Great, write 'em down. Now, what does this have to do with equality? Well, before we attempt to define something like *equality*, which is so broadly interpreted, and especially biased in the realm of politics and the popular media, it is important to get a sense of your own personal paradigm on the matter.

A *paradigm* consists of the assumptions that you make, the perceptions that you have and the values that you assign in regard to a specific concept such as equality. In other words, it represents your pattern of thinking on a subject. Your responses to the questions in the previous paragraph reveal a portion of the paradigm that you hold concerning equality, especially as it relates to those who are rich versus those who are poor. Now, let's consider yet another story and see how your paradigm holds up.

THE MAKING OF A GLASS KING

Harold A. McMaster was born on a tenant farm near Deshler, Ohio, in 1916. He was one of thirteen children, and unfortunately he and his family were very well-acquainted with poverty. Nevertheless, when Harold was six years old, his father was able to give him his first set of tools, and by the age of eight, he had already built his first pieces of farm machinery. As a result of his creativity and innovation, and fueled by his early success, Harold continued to build and invent. By the age of ten he had produced a threshing machine that husked corn, and by the age of twelve he was already building car motors. In spite of his humble beginnings, young McMaster was, indeed, becoming quite the inventor.[1]

Realizing his need for a college education in order to pursue his dreams, Harold enrolled in Defiance College and later transferred to Ohio State University, where he earned degrees in arts, nuclear physics, astronomy, and mathematics. Upon graduation in 1940, he went to work for Libbey-Owens-Ford, where he applied his creative genius to the war effort by inventing a rear-vision periscope for fighter aircraft, and a method of de-icing aircraft windshields. By 1948, McMaster had left LOF in order to start his own company, Permaglass. Within three years, Permaglass had become the leading supplier of glass plates for television sets. Success continued for the hardworking McMaster, and by 1958, bending and tempering glass for the auto industry had become his main business. But by 1971, he had merged his company with Guardian Industries out of Detroit and left the company in order to start yet another.[2]

His next venture, with partner and fellow inventor Norman Nitschke, was known as Glasstech. It did not take long before development was underway for a prototype of what was to be a revolutionary new machine used for the production of tempered glass. So, what's the big deal about tempered glass? Well, consider this:

> The molecular profile of glass portrays it as a material five times stronger than steel. Internal defects and irregularities that occur during production limit its actual strength. A process for making high-quality strengthened, or tempered, glass had been the Holy Grail of glass technology for more than two thousand years. Roman Pliny the Elder wrote that it would be more valuable than gold. Tempered glass is essential for windows in skyscrapers, home patio doors, shower doors, and other structures. [In addition to its strength, tempered glass also] breaks into crumbs [when broken] and is less likely to injure people than the razor-sharp shards that fly when ordinary glass breaks. Mr. McMaster's research and development team at Glasstech, Inc., found that Holy Grail.[3]

When they finally finished, they had succeeded in developing a machine that could produce the world's strongest and clearest tempered glass. It is estimated that nearly 80 percent of the world's automotive glass and approximately 50 percent of its architectural glass is now manufactured by these machines.[4]

To the end of his days, McMaster continued to press forward with new ideas and sought to improve upon old ones, the last of which included his continued development of rotary engines, as well as groundbreaking work in the field of solar energy. By the time of his death in 2003, McMaster held more than one hundred patents in relation to glass bending and tempering, solar energy, and rotary engines. And while he was extremely well-known in the glass industry, he was equally well-known for his generosity. Harold McMaster and his wife, Helen, started various foundations and donated millions of dollars to libraries, universities, hospitals, and other institutions throughout northwest Ohio and southeastern Michigan. It should also be noted that his generosity went far beyond the capacity to quantify, as it is said that McMaster donated to society much of the needed technology for commercial-scale solar energy, receiving very little in return.[5]

PARADIGM SHIFT

So, what does this story do to your paradigm? Does it change any of your answers from earlier? For years, our politicians and "popular" media have sold us the line that "the poor are *always* oppressed by the rich," or "rich people *do not* know what it is like to do manual labor and work hard," and that "the rich *never* pay their fair share of taxes." Although there are many more aspects that we could explore, these three seem to be the "hot buttons" around which many people build their paradigms. So, let us weigh the truth of these statements and see how they hold up.

Are rich people *always* oppressing poor people? According to *Merriam-Webster*, to "oppress" literally means "to crush or burden by abuse of power or authority."[6] Okay, so let us consider the following question for a moment: Are all rich people in positions of power or authority? Either by virtue of the fact that many of them own businesses or have the capacity to influence others in authority with generous "donations" of various types, most of the rich *are* in a position of some authority. But this begs another question: Are all of them abusing their power and authority? It does not appear that Mr. McMaster did. In fact, by virtue of his ingenuity and labor, thousands of people have been employed throughout the years. The same could be said of most business owners in the private sector. Without their investments in small companies, many of us would be unemployed. Fine.

So the next question is this: Can they employ thousands of people and still abuse their power? Yes, absolutely. However, just because they *can* does not mean that they *do*. If Harold McMaster is an example of a rich person who did *not* oppress the poor, but on the contrary put them to work so that they could earn a paycheck and better themselves, and he willingly donated the technology for the advancement of all in society, then indeed, rich people do *not* always oppress the poor. Some do. Some do not. What we need to remember is that *oppression can occur anywhere that people are placed in a position of power and authority.* The "popular" media hold a position of authority, do they not? How about politicians? How about the workplace foreman or office manager? What about the head of a home? *Power and authority exist on many levels, and so does oppression.* It is *not* reserved only for the rich.

Next, do rich people know what it is like to do manual labor and work hard? Obviously McMaster did. You cannot live on a farm, build a set of farm machinery, or put together car engines without knowing what it is like to do hard manual labor! In fact, it could be argued that a vast majority of the world's billionaires know the value of hard work and manual labor, as a fair majority of them became billionaires from the ground up. According to *Forbes* magazine:

> Almost two-thirds of the world's 946 billionaires made their fortunes from scratch, relying on grit and determination, and not good genes. Fifty of these self-made tycoons are college or high school dropouts.[7]

While it may be true that some of this nation's *rich* have never worked a hard day of labor in their lives, the same could be said of *some* of our *poor* people, who do nothing more than "sponge" off of friends, family, and the government. You do not have to be rich to avoid hard labor—you can simply be lazy.

Finally, do the rich ever really pay their fair share of the tax burden in America? If I listen to the "popular" media, or even the current "buzz" in Washington, D.C., the answer would be a resounding "no—the rich never pay their fair share!" However, let me share with you the truth on the subject according to the government's own tax information—no "spin," no manipulation, just the numbers.

To make things simple let's look at things this way: the total amount of taxes paid in the year 2007 will be represented by 100 pigs:

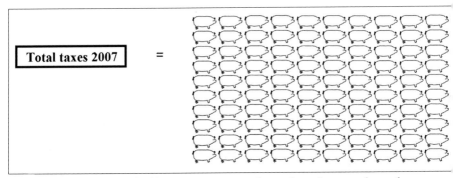

And 1% of all wage earners (people who work and receive a paycheck) will be represented by one person:

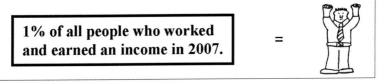

According to the IRS, in 2007 the top (richest) one percent of wage earners, those who made the most money, paid over 40% of all taxes collected:

The top (richest) 10% combined paid over 71% of all taxes collected:

And the top (richest) 50% of all wage earners combined paid over 97% of all of the federal income tax money collected for the year (above and below pictures combined)...

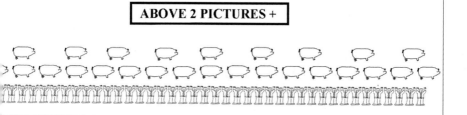

...while the bottom 50% of all wage earners paid a mere 2.89% of all taxes collected:[8]

Which in truth is only about 18 of those little men are holding those 2.89% pigs due to the fact that over 32% of the bottom 50% pay no income taxes at all.[9]

Many of these paid in the full amount owed, but they got it all back as well. In fact, according to IRS statistics, the percentage of taxes paid by the bottom 50 percent has steadily declined from 7.05 percent in 1980 to 2.89 percent by 2007, while at the same time the percentage of federal income taxes paid by the top one percent of all wage earners has more than doubled, going from 19.05 percent in 1980 up to 40.42 percent by 2007.[10] Not only that, but since the year 2000, the percentage of people who are not required to pay any income taxes at all, based upon their being on the lower end of the income scale, has increased by 59 percent![11]

Again, so what and who cares? In other words, contrary to popular opinion, the rich not only pay their fair share and more of the tax burden, but their taxes have also more than doubled over the past three decades, while the taxes of the poor have steadily declined and have even been cut in half in that same time period.

Now, granted, this is not the complete picture of who pays or does not pay or, for that matter, who cheats on their taxes, etc. However, it should be enough to help us recognize a few things. First of all, while the rich have been demonized by many of our politicians and the "popular" media for causing all of our nation's economic problems, at least some of the information they have given us (as it relates to these facts above) has been nothing but lies. As we discussed in chapter 2, this is why it is so critical to start checking the facts and not simply believe everything we're fed by our media and politicians (whether we like them, trust them, voted for them, or not).

Second, the rich and the poor have a lot more in common than what many in the media or our government want us to realize. *Both* have the capacity to oppress or liberate others. *Both* have the capacity to work hard or not at all. And while we have not discussed it in detail, *both* are saddled with a government that is out of control as it relates to the spending of their tax dollars!

Third and finally, I suggest to you that many of our politicians and many in the "popular" media are perhaps *purposely* trying to drive a wedge between the rich and the poor, between black and white, between Christian and non-Christian, and between any other groups that can be divided in this nation. Why would they do that? *Because when you have a house divided, and you are in charge...you can do just about anything you want.*

EQUALITY...

So then, what does all of this have to do with equality? I'm glad you asked! Our Declaration of Independence states the following:

We hold these truths to be self-evident, that all men are created equal, that they are endowed by their Creator with certain unalienable Rights, that among these are Life, Liberty and the pursuit of Happiness.[12]

Equality is not a subjective thing, but rather a concrete and inherent trait of all human beings. We were created equal. To be created equal implies that equality is not a thing to be grasped or taken away from an individual. On the contrary, it is a divine quality placed within us. What exactly is this quality? As Thomas Jefferson penned so eloquently, and as our Founding Fathers agreed, it is that attribute of humanity that compels us to exercise our God-given rights to life, liberty, and the pursuit of happiness, regardless of our station in life.

Life. We all possess a right to *live* and draw breath, and to take this basic right away from us is wrong. I can *choose* to place myself in harm's way, to commit a crime deserving of capital punishment, or perhaps even to lose my life as a result of an accident based on something foolish I have done. Nevertheless, as long as I choose to honor and respect the rights of others to do the same, I have a right to live and breathe.

Liberty. So long as we do not infringe upon the life and liberty of others, we are free to choose, or rather, we have the liberty to do as we please. We can *choose* to work hard, or not. We can *choose* to take big or small financial risks in the hopes of accumulating wealth, or not. We can *choose* to give great amounts or small amounts of our income to others, or not. We can *choose* to reject God, or enter into relationship with Him, and so on, and so on.

Happiness. What is your definition of *happiness*?

Regardless of what it is, you have the right to pursue it, as long as it does not infringe upon the basic rights of others. You do not have the right to have happiness or whatever you want just given to you; rather, you have the right to choose what you wish to pursue.

Equality, then, is the right that all men and women share: to live, to choose, and to pursue whatever they desire as long as it does not infringe upon others' rights to do the same. We may not like the choices that others make, but those choices are theirs to make. For better or for worse, we are a product of our choices. We are not entitled to have lots of money, nor are we entitled to have the wealth of the rich redistributed to us. Yet we can choose to pursue wealth, and we should be confident that when we finally reach that goal, that it will not be taken from us and given to others in an attempt to be fair. Also, not everything is about wealth. For instance, not every child is entitled to or deserving of an A in school, but those who wish to do so can pursue an A. Consider this:

> Socialists are attempting to create a "classless so-ciety" in which all people share equally in all material possessions. They want no gap between the have and have nots. But if there was no gap, we would no longer be rewarding people for their wisdom and dili-gence. There should be some rich/poor gap, because there is a wise-and-diligent/foolish-and-lazy gap.[13]

Are all of the rich, therefore, wise and diligent? No, some of them are foolish and lazy. Are all of the poor foolish and lazy? No, again, some of them are wise and diligent. However, take a rich man who is foolish and lazy, and he will not be rich for long. Conversely, take a poor man who is wise and diligent, and given time, he will not remain poor! The bottom line is this:

> EQUALITY has nothing to do with what we possess physically or externally… It has everything to do with what we possess internally or spiritually.

It is just one more area of common ground that we share, regardless of our financial worth.

I pray you would carefully consider your own personal mind-set as it relates to equality. And as you do so, I also pray that these truths would become "self-evident" in this nation once again.

RECOMMENDED READING

Harold R. Eberle, *Compassionate Capitalism, A Judeo-Christian Value*, 2010.

—The topics of equality and capitalism are intimately related. Again, good stuff; check it out!

Notes

1 *The Toledo Blade*, "Obituaries," August 26, 2003. Accessed on September 13, 2010. http://www.toledoblade.com/apps/pbcs.dll/article?AID=/20030826/NEWS13/108260085.

2 Ibid.

3 Ibid.

4 Ibid.

5 Ibid.

6 Merriam-Webster, "oppress," 2010. Accessed on September 13, 2010. http://www.merriam-webster.com/dictionary/oppress.

7 Tatiana Serafin, "Rags to Riches Billionaires," *Forbes* magazine online, June 26, 2007. Accessed on September 13, 2010. http://www.forbes.com/2007/06/22/billionaires-gates-winfrey-biz-cz_ts_0626rags2riches.html.

8 Gerald Prante, "Fiscal Facts: Summary of Latest Federal Individual Income Tax Data," *Tax Foundation*, July 30, 2009. Accessed on September 15, 2010. http://www.taxfoundation.org/news/show/250.html.

9 Scott A. Hodge, "Fiscal Facts: Record Numbers of People Paying No Income Tax: Over 50 Million 'Nonpayers' Include Families Making over $50,000," *Tax Foundation*, March 10, 2010. Accessed on September 15, 2010. http://www.taxfoundation.org/publications/show/25962.html.

10 Prante.

11 Hodge.

12 The Declaration of Independence.

13 Harold R. Eberle, *Compassionate Capitalism: A Judeo-Christian Value* (Yakima: Worldcast Publishing, 2010), 96.

~ Thirteen ~

FOUNDATIONAL MORALITY

As I was praying about the lead-in for this chapter, God dropped the words *Hansel and Gretel* into my mind. I searched high and low for some cool hidden attribute that related to the story of Hansel and Gretel, or the Grimm Brothers, but try as I might, I could not come up with anything. For that matter, I was not even sure whether I remembered or had ever heard the entire story before. So I sat down, found the original story from the Grimm Brothers on the Internet, and began to read it. What a great story! As I read the story in its entirety for the first time and then began to pray about it over the next several days, God gave me some new insights, interesting parallels, and the relevance to the things that He had already given me to share in this chapter.

The Grimm Brothers most assuredly did not intend it for this purpose; nevertheless, I believe that this story is a beautiful prophetic picture of where we have been, where we are, and where we are called to go as a nation. So you can go out and buy a book that contains the full story (see the recommended books at the end of the chapter), look up the full story online, or simply enjoy my abridged but unadulterated version of *Hansel and Gretel*.

NOT THE STORY I KNEW

Once upon a time, there lived a woodcutter, his wife, and his two children, Hansel and Gretel. Times were very hard and they had very little to eat, for a great famine had spread across the land. Anxious about how he would feed and care for his entire family, the woodcutter lamented to his wife, "Whatever shall I do?" His wife, the stepmother to the man's children, answered in this manner: "Early tomorrow morning we shall take the children into the forest, where it is thickest. There we will light a fire for them, give each of them one more piece of bread, and then we shall go to our work and leave them alone. They will not find the way home again, and we shall be rid of them."

"No, wife," said the man. "They are the children whom I love dearly. Most assuredly the wild animals will find them and tear them to pieces."

"Oh! You fool," said she, "then we must all four die of hunger, you may as well plane the planks for our coffins," and she left him no peace until he agreed.

Now, being so hungry that they could not sleep, the children had overheard everything. Gretel began to despair. "Hansel, what will we do? For surely we shall die in the woods."

But Hansel quietly reassured his sister, "Don't worry, I'll think of something." And when his parents had gone off to bed and were fast asleep, Hansel snuck downstairs, quietly went outside, and filled his pockets with pebbles that shone and glittered in the moonlight like real silver coins. He then went back inside, lay down, and comforted his sister once again, "Don't worry, little sister, sleep in peace. God will not forsake us."

When daybreak came, they awoke to the belittling tones of their stepmother, telling them to get dressed, for they were going to the forest to fetch wood for the day. They were each given a piece of bread to last the day, and then together they set off into the forest to fetch wood. When they had reached the middle of the forest, they were instructed by their father to pile up wood and light a fire so they would not get cold. The woodcutter and his wife then told the children to stay by the fire while they went off into the forest to cut wood. So the children sat by the fire and nibbled on their bread from time to time. Soon, they were both fast asleep. When they awoke, it was dark and they knew that, indeed, they had been left in the forest to die.

Gretel immediately began to panic. "How are we ever going to get out of the forest now?" she lamented. Then Hansel told her about the silver pebbles that he had gone out to fetch the night before and how, unknown to their parents, he had been dropping them all along the path since the time they had left home that morning. All they had to do now was to wait for the moon to rise high overhead, and the silver pebbles glowing in the moonlight would lead them home.

Sure enough, the moon rose and the pebbles shone. By daybreak Hansel and Gretel had found their way home, and their father was overjoyed to see them, for it had broken his heart to leave them.

Not long afterward, there again came a famine that spread across the land. Once more the children overheard their stepmother complaining one night, "We have no more food. The children have got to go. We will take them deeper into the forest this time, so that they cannot possibly return."

So once again, when the parents were fast asleep, Hansel

crept downstairs intending to fill his pockets with silver pebbles as he had before. However, this time his stepmother had locked the door fast, and he could not get out. Nevertheless, he comforted his sister saying, "Don't cry, Gretel, sleep and be comforted. The good God will help us."

So, early the next morning, the children were hustled out of bed, each given a piece of bread for the day, and once more led out into the forest. As before, they awoke at the end of the day to find themselves abandoned deep in the forest.

"Whatever shall we do?" Gretel despaired once again. Hansel proceeded to tell her how this time, since the door was locked and he could not get any stones, he had taken his bread, crumbled it up, and had dropped the crumbs along the path so they could find their way home.

Well, the moon rose and shone brightly upon the ground, but there were no crumbs to be seen, for the birds of the air had come along behind poor Hansel and devoured his trail.

Nevertheless, Hansel encouraged his sister and said, "We will soon find our way out." But they did not. They walked the entire night and all the next day, but they did not find their way out of the forest. They were very tired and very hungry, for all they had found to eat were a few berries.

Days passed, and the children wandered deeper and deeper into the woods while searching for their father's house. By noon of the third day, they came upon a beautiful snow-white bird that alighted on the tree before them and began singing a delightful tune, to which the children stood still and listened to. When its song was done, it spread its wings and flew away before them, and the children decided to follow it. Before long, the children came upon a clearing and found the bird sitting upon the roof of a charming little house. As they drew near, they discovered that the house was actually built of bread, covered with cakes, and had windows made of clear sugar. Immediately the children set to devouring as much of that little house as they could, for they had not eaten in days. But not long afterward, in the middle of their feasting, the door suddenly swung open to reveal a woman who appeared to be older than the hills. She kindly invited them in for a good meal, and prepared beds for each, for it was obvious that the children were exhausted. The children thought they were in heaven and they gave no further thought to danger after gratefully accepting the generous offer of this seemingly kind old woman.

Soon they were fast asleep, and the kind, generous old woman began to scheme how she would fatten them up so she could eat them, for in reality she was nothing more than an evil old witch.

Early the next morning, as she enticed herself with the thought of dining on the plump little children, the evil witch grabbed Hansel with her gnarled hand, abruptly dragged him to the small stable out back, and locked him in a cage. She then proceeded to wake Gretel, saying, "Get up, you lazy child, fetch some water and begin to cook for your brother, who I locked away in the stable. You shall cook for him and make him fat, and then I will eat him."

Greatly distressed and fearing for her brother's life as well as her own, Gretel did as the witch commanded. Each morning the witch would go to the stable and command Hansel, "Stretch out your finger that I may feel if you will soon be fat." And each morning Hansel would take a small bone from the cage and stick it out for the witch to feel, for the witch had very poor eyesight.

After four weeks of the same routine, the witch once again felt the "finger" that Hansel had given her to assess. Outraged and astonished by the fact that this little boy appeared no fatter now than he had been four weeks ago, the witch became impatient and enraged. She would wait no longer. She yelled for Gretel to wake up, and "Bring some water for the cauldron, for today I shall kill your brother and eat him."

Gretel awoke, ran out to meet the witch, as she had been commanded to do, and upon seeing the dire situation that she and her brother were now in, she exclaimed, "Dear God, do help us!"

"First we shall bake," said the old hag. "I have already heated the oven and kneaded the dough." She quickly and abruptly pushed poor Gretel, who by now was beside herself in tears, nearer to the oven, from which flames of fire were now darting.

"Climb in," said the witch, "and see if it is properly heated," for once Gretel had come near enough, the witch intended to push her in, close the door, and bake her so as to be eaten along with her brother. Though distraught over her brother, young Gretel was well aware of what the witch had in mind, and she pretended not to understand what the witch was asking her to do.

As the witch proceeded to show her how to climb up and stick her head into the oven, Gretel seized the opportunity and forcefully pushed the old witch the rest of the way into the oven, closed the door, and locked it tight. The witch let out a bloodcurdling screech that soon trailed off, as she was cooked by her own evil scheme.

Gretel then ran to the stable, threw open the door, and

cried to her brother, "Hansel, we are saved. The old witch is dead." When she released him, Hansel sprang from the cage, embraced his sister, and kissed her as tears of joy ran down their little faces. Since there was no longer any reason to fear, the children returned to the house one last time, only to discover chests full of jewels and pearls in every corner of the house. Upon seeing them, they began to stuff their pockets with as much as they could hold.

With pockets full, Hansel turned to his sister and said, "Very good, we need to be off now." They left the cottage and walked for two hours, before coming to a great stretch of water with no bridge, no ferry, and no way to cross. The only thing upon the water appeared to be a little white duck.

At Gretel's request, the little white duck came over and carried them safely, one at time, to the other side of the great expanse of water. As they continued to walk on from there, they began to notice that the forest was growing more and more familiar. It was not long before they suddenly spotted the chimney of their father's house. They quickly ran to the house, and upon finding their father inside, they wrapped their arms around his neck and wouldn't let go.

The man hadn't known a single happy hour since he had abandoned his children in the forest. Their stepmother, however, was now dead. Gretel emptied her apron until pearls and precious stones ran about the room, and Hansel emptied his pockets, one handful after another, to add to them. Overjoyed and with their sorrows now behind them, they went on to live together in perfect happiness.[1]

THE LEGALITY OF MORALITY

First of all, let me say that this is not the quaint little story that I recall growing up with. However, it *is* the version the Grimm Brothers intended, and quite honestly I like it even better.

Second, I have a few questions: How do you feel about parents sacrificing their own children in order to save themselves? And what do you think about the consumption of little children? Aside from a few tongue-in-cheek responses or perhaps some off-color jokes from burnt-out parents, I suspect that the overwhelming response to these questions is that these things are unquestionably wrong. This being the case, we must begin this discussion by admitting that in this world, there exist many things that are definitely *right*, and things that are definitely *wrong*.

Morality is simply our system of conduct (or rather, how we believe we should act or behave), based upon our idea of right and wrong. For the vast majority of Americans, including our Founding Fathers, our sense of morality has been drawn from the Judeo-Christian system of values, better known to most as the Ten Commandments. Yet in fairness, not all agree with or adhere to this value system. So, how do we determine what guidelines to embrace when laying down the laws of the land?

Before we can effectively do that, we must first deal with a statement that is frequently tossed out anytime this discussion comes up, namely that "morality cannot be legislated." In essence, this says that the consideration of morality has no place in determining which laws should be enacted and enforced in governing the people of a nation, or their respective states. Yet correct me if I'm wrong: It would appear that we have already done so by enacting laws that deter murder, theft, and rape, to name but a few. This being true, it is then apparent that morality does and has, in fact, played a role in molding our legal system. If we can accept this much, then the next question is this: How much of a role does and should morality play in the making of our laws? For example, what if most people believe that it is wrong to pick one's nose in public? Should we begin enacting legislation to run those public pickers to the nearest jail? No, that is absurd! So, where is the line that needs to be drawn when it comes to enacting legislation based upon right and wrong?

It lies with the primary role and purpose of our federal government in establishing laws in the first place—to secure the rights of life, liberty, and the pursuit of happiness. The federal government and morality share this common purpose and desire for the individual in their primary goals, as well as the nation as a whole. Both are needed for this nation to stay on course and to continue in the fullness of her God-given mandate. Within this point of tension lies the proper relationship between Lord and liberty, God and country. Therefore, *the degree to which morality should influence the laws of this nation is the extent to which it assists in making laws that keep others from infringing upon our inalienable rights to life, liberty, and the pursuit of happiness.*

For example, murder is considered *wrong* by most, but the fact that it *infringes* upon another person's right to life necessitates laws prohibiting it. Public nose-picking, on the other hand, does not interfere with or infringe upon the rights of others—unless someone is assaulting another with what came out of their nose for some strange reason. No law needed; it is just gross. Therefore, since we have concluded that morality does and should have an influence on laws that are established in this nation, does this then imply that all things that are legal are also morally right? No.

Consider abortion. It is a legal act that is morally wrong. I know, it is also the big fat *elephant* in the middle of the room that we are supposed to pretend is not there and therefore we should not talk about. Let me also say here that this is in no way a statement of judgment or condemnation upon those who have had or performed abortions, or those who disagree with me. I have made more than my fair share of mistakes in life—the last thing I want to do with anyone else is to point a finger of judgment. In God's economy, there is always mercy and forgiveness. It's why I love Him so much—because I've been forgiven so much! However, I have never been too good at ignoring big fat elephants, so let's consider the abortion question within the framework we have just laid out. In fact, we will even consider it from the pro-abortion point of view, which essentially states that the freedom of choice should be legal.

In order to do so, our next step is to line this statement up with our purpose for establishing laws (which is to keep others from infringing upon our inalienable rights to life, liberty, and the pursuit of happiness). When we do that, the abortionist point of view must be stated as follows: that the freedom of choice should be legal so long as it does not infringe upon another's rights to life, liberty, or pursuit of happiness. So, inevitably, it comes back to the question, when does life begin? From a secular standpoint alone, we teach our kids in Biology 101 about the "life" that exists in single-cell organisms. A fertilized egg is no different. It possesses the same characteristics of life and then it divides into two cells...then four cells...then eight... It doesn't take long, and in just three weeks little eyes are formed, and so on.

Amazing. Just ask many of the secular pro-choice activists, as they are often the same group of people who are lobbying for laws to protect the eggs (unborn creatures?) of bald eagles, spotted owls, and every other endangered egg-laying creature. Why protect those eggs unless you are conceding that they do, in fact, contain "life"? Ironically enough, to them it is "life" when a creature is endangered; it appears to be just "tissue" when it is inconvenient.

Are there traumatic situations that sometimes surround conception? Unfortunately, yes, and the victims of such experiences need to be treated with the utmost love, empathy, and support. But life is life. Rape victims aside, if you do not want to take the chance or have the responsibility of being pregnant and carrying a baby to full-term, then don't have sex, period. Go ahead and use contraceptives, get your tubes tied, whatever—try to prevent it all you want, that *is* your right. But once conception has occurred, life begins; we have made our choice and we now need to live with the consequences of our actions like mature adults. You want pro-choice? Fine. Just make those choices before conception takes place.

Once conceived, that human life now has the same rights as the rest of us. Abortion is not about whether a woman has a right to do what she desires with her own body; it is about whether or not she has the right to kill the American citizen whom she now carries inside of her. For now, abortion is legal, but it certainly is not moral.

A PROPHETIC PICTURE

A prophetic picture is one that illustrates, from God's perspective, what was, what is, and what He desires to come to pass. As I read through the story of *Hansel and Gretel*, God began to reveal the story to me as a prophetic picture of our nation. So, combined with some further study of my own, the following is the spirit of what He was revealing.

To begin with, Hansel is a form of the name *Hans*, which literally means "God's grace." A basic definition of *grace* is "God's unmerited favor," or rather, "gifts that He freely gives that cannot be earned." The name *Gretel* means "pearl." As I read, God spoke to me that Gretel in the story represented the present generation of people in this nation; we are *God's pearl*.

The story speaks of a generation of people (represented by the father) who knew what was right, yet against their better judgment, they allowed some from among them (represented by the stepmother) to enact socialistic laws and policies in order to save their own generation. Nonetheless (like the stepmother's plans), these decisions would have far-reaching and detrimental effects on future generations (Gretel). Like the stepmother's plan in the story, it was soon discovered that the socialist policies were not foolproof, and that people were still very resistant to the concept of socialism. For as long as morality (represented by the shiny pebbles—provided by "God's grace," or Hansel) was still taught in the schools, future generations (Gretel) would always have a desire and a way to thwart the socialist agenda. So they (like the stepmother) closed the door and locked it, removing God, and dependable morality (the shiny pebbles) from the public schools completely. With the old forms of morality gone, they were soon replaced with a "new morality" (bread crumbs—the only thing available from the stepmother), which would not be enough to sustain future generations (Gretel) or enable them to return home to their constitutional foundation and God's original design. And for a while, their plans succeeded, for they did not even consider the possibility that God's grace (Hansel) would be sufficient enough to guide future generations out of the deepest political muck and mire (represented by the forest) into which they had just been led and abandoned. For the longest time, future generations (Gretel) just went along with the status quo and were content with what was offered (the witch's house/food/bed), until one day, they woke up and realized that God's grace (Hansel) had been taken away from them as a result of their choices.

Yet, these questions remain for this generation: Will we choose to overthrow (by engaging in the democratic process and elections) the ruling royalty of politicians and leadership (the witch) that currently plagues this country and seeks to destroy God's grace? Will we say no to our selfish nature by refusing all of their free handouts and bribes (goodies offered by the witch)? Will we refuse the "new morality" (that of the witch and the stepmother) of socialism and its counterparts as a substitute for true morality, and return to the living God of our forefathers? Or will we roll over, climb into the oven, and die (thus bringing about the end of a free nation)?

God's grace is waiting and available...the choice is now ours.

RECOMMENDED READING

1. Grimm Brothers, the, *The Complete Grimm's Fairy Tales*, 1972.

—Hands down, the unabridged version is far superior to my scaled-down rendition. Plus, theirs has cool illustrations.

2. Oliver DeMille, *A Thomas Jefferson Education*, 2006.

—I cannot say that I am in lockstep agreement with everything stated in this book, but it is very well-written, and it highlights some core elements that are greatly lacking, or in some cases altogether missing, from much of our current public and private educational systems.

Notes

1 Grimm Brothers, The, "Hansel and Gretel," in *The Complete Grimm's Fairy Tales* (New York: Random House, 1972).

~ Fourteen ~

SEPARATION ANXIETY

It's time to address the primary burning issue that inevitably comes up when an author attempts to combine God and government in one book: What about the *separation of church and state*? Good question, and we will look at it in its proper context in a moment. But before we do so, let us first observe how this issue was dealt with by another nation—a nation that suffered through the trials and tribulations of revolution just shortly after the American Revolution had been won.

A REVOLUTIONARY SIBLING

Louis XVI was only twenty years old when he was crowned the king of France. He ascended to the royal throne and reigned from 1774 through 1792, during the height of the American Revolution. It was *his* France that played a key role in the battle of Yorktown in 1781, where the British finally surrendered, thus helping to secure American independence. The irony of that event was that while Louis XVI was instrumental in assisting the American dream to become a reality, he found himself unable to attain any such dream of liberty and prosperity for his own native France.

Many factors led to revolutionary unrest in France at that time. Louis XVI was faced with the challenges of an enormous national debt and a rapidly deteriorating public opinion, due in part to an ever-increasing tax burden on the people. In addition to this, many families lived in fear for their own welfare, as widespread famine afflicted large segments of the population with death and disease. A vast and growing majority believed that Louis was unfit and ill-prepared to rule the nation of France; he was young, indecisive, and untested. While he was basically an honest man with good intentions, he lacked the necessary vision or, at the very least, the capacity to articulate and implement what vision he may have had in order to solve the country's mounting difficulties. The result was a bloody revolution that tore the nation of France apart, separating it into several political factions, and ultimately led to his death at the guillotine in January of 1793. Since that time, France has seen the rise and fall of two empires, two subsequent monarchies, and five different Republics.[1]

While it could be argued that both the American and French Revolutions began as a result of the same spirit of independence, one very significant difference exists between the two: the role of Divine Providence (aka God). With the fall of the French empire, relations between the French revolutionaries and the Church were severely damaged and became strained at best. It could even be argued that the Church had it coming as they had contributed to the poverty of the people by imposing a *mandatory* 10 percent tax (tithe) on all of France's citizens. (Unquestionably Church leadership has not always done things correctly throughout the ages, even in spite of her best efforts.) Nevertheless, this was a point of separation that amounted to the Church being tolerated by future generations but never again being an integral part of any new governmental systems in France, as it was with the new American government.[2] The Americans had made it clear in their First Amendment that they would not establish a government-controlled religion (in other words, a government denomination) in which every citizen would be obliged to participate. However, they would encourage America's citizens to worship God, and they would structure their government in such a way as to honor God. They even went so far as to declare their dependence upon Him for their independence. France, on the other hand, seemed to make a clear break from God with few exceptions and chose instead a firm dependence upon themselves and none other.

What has been the difference between the two nations in the centuries since? France has had nine different changes in its governmental system since the time of her revolution, in contrast with America's one. Still, some would argue my viewpoint regarding the First Amendment, as well as question what is meant by the phrase "separation of church and state." So, let us briefly look at the two.

INTERPRETIVE DANCE

First of all, let us begin with the phrase "wall of separation between the church and the state." It is *not* found in our Constitution, but it is nonetheless looked to as the definitive statement that removes all forms of religion from governmental programs, public schools, and public arenas. So, where did this phrase come from? Let's take a look:

The phrase "wall of separation between the church and the state" was originally coined by Thomas Jefferson in a letter to the Danbury Baptists on January 1, 1802. His purpose in this letter was to assuage the fears of the Danbury, Connecticut Baptists, and so he told them that this wall had been erected to protect them. The metaphor was used exclusively to keep the state out of the church's business, not to keep the church out of the state's business.[3]

History can rarely be interpreted or fully understood in light of today's language and definitions alone. To comprehensively understand what our forefathers laid out for us, we must view their statements in the full context from which they were taken. This means researching the historical letters, speeches, conversations, and the like from which these statements were taken, in order to ascertain a better sense of what was intended.[4] When we do this with the phrase in question, it is quite clear that no such wall between Church and state was ever intended or even existed, except for the express purpose of protecting the religious establishment. That notwithstanding, much has been written on the subject since (both pro and con), and I encourage you to do some research of your own. Check out the recommended reading given at the end of this chapter.

Second, let us look at the First Amendment itself: "Congress shall make no law respecting an establishment of religion, or prohibiting the free exercise thereof." The word "respecting" is not used in the sense of *showing respect for* your elders. It literally means "*with respect to*."[5] So, let's read it again with this change: "Congress shall make no law [with respect to] an establishment of religion..." When you further take the time to read the original drafts of this amendment, and the resulting discussions that took place leading up to the final draft,[6] you will be hard-pressed to interpret this phrase in any other way than that our founders simply wanted to avoid the establishment of a state-run church (or denomination). In addition, they did not want the government to place any restrictions upon, nor pass any laws that might interfere with, religion.

Now, some attorneys may tell us at this point that because we do not have law degrees, we have no business trying to interpret the law or the Constitution. What a ridiculous idea. We do not need a law degree in order to research and understand history, or the English language in its proper context. The Church tried the same thing in the Middle Ages, when they told the common person that only *trained* clergy could read and fully understand God's Word (the Bible), and that, too, was completely wrong.

> All men who have turned out worth anything have
> had the chief hand in their own education.
> —*Sir Walter Scott*

Lawyers and clergymen are very helpful; they have certainly sacrificed much to attain their skill and expertise, and my comments are not meant to disparage either—I am a member of the clergy myself. Yet, as it turns out, the Church was just being an overcontrolling mother hen at that time, and *some* of the clergy did not want the people to comprehend the Bible, knowing that once they did, those in power in the Church would hold less power to control and manipulate them. The Bible has since been translated into nearly every known language, and it is being read, studied, and comprehended by many without college degrees. The same is true with attorneys. Some of them do not want you to comprehend the law because once you do, they will have less power to control and manipulate you. For that matter, the same could be said concerning nearly every profession. Nevertheless, there are still some who would say that the intent of the First Amendment was to keep religion out of the public arena completely including our schools, politics, and government. So, let's consider one final angle.

What exactly constitutes "religion"? Strictly speaking, the word *religion* means "a cause, principle, or system of beliefs held to with ardor and faith."[7] So, if we want to concede the argument and interpret the intent of the First Amendment as being to keep religion out of public schools, politics, and government, then let us also be consistent with applying our definition of the word *religion*. According to the definition of *religion*, evolution should not be taught in public schools. Both evolution and Creation-science have some scientific evidence to make their case, but in the end, neither can be conclusively proven and each is, therefore, a system of beliefs that constitutes religion. Atheism is also a belief system—it "believes" that all religious belief systems are wrong and that there is no God, also by definition a "religion." Global warming is another unproven theory; it is a system of beliefs and therefore—a "religion." Hence, in the end it would appear that our choice in this matter boils down to one of two things: Either we believe that freedom from religion was the intent of our Founders and we begin ridding this nation of all religious infringement by applying this principle across the board, or perhaps we simply need to begin applying prudence (aka common sense) and become more diligent at calling out and questioning the intent and agenda of those in the media, in the judiciary, or in public office who would choose to apply it so unilaterally.

AN IMPARTIAL OBSERVER

The way we live from day to day is the evidence of our hearts' intent. In other words, our actions speak louder than our words. If this is true, then the intent of what our Founding Fathers wrote should have been quite evident in the customs, policies, laws, and the very fabric of the society itself during our first century as a nation. Therefore, I would leave you with some observations made by a famous French statesman, historian, and social philosopher by the name of Alexis de Tocqueville, after he toured America in 1831 for the first time. At the young age of twenty-six, he had already witnessed several changes in France's governmental system, and he observed firsthand how his country had been ravaged by its effects. Perhaps the observations of one who has seen the downside of revolution can better help us comprehend the intent of our Founders and appreciate the beauty and wonder of what they were able to accomplish. Consider:

> Upon my arrival in the United States, the religious aspect of the country was the first thing that struck my attention; and the longer I stayed there, the more I perceived the great political consequences resulting from this new state of things.
>
> In France I had almost always seen the spirit of religion and the spirit of freedom marching in opposite directions. But in America I found they were inti-

mately united and that they reigned in common over the same country.

Religion in America...must be regarded as the foremost of the political institutions of that country; for if it does not impart a taste for freedom, it facilitates the use of it. Indeed, it is in this same point of view that the inhabitants of the United States themselves look upon religious belief.

I do not know whether all Americans have a sincere faith in their religion—for who can search the human heart?—But I am certain that they hold it to be indispensable to the maintenance of republican institutions. This opinion is not peculiar to a class of citizens or a party, but it belongs to the whole nation and to every rank of society.

The sects that exist in the United States are innumerable. They all differ in respect to the worship which is due to the Creator; but they all agree in respect to the duties which are due from man to man.

Each sect adores the Deity in its own peculiar manner, but all sects preach the same moral law in the name of God...

Moreover, all the sects of the United States are comprised within the great unity of Christianity, and Christian morality is everywhere the same.

In the United States the sovereign authority is religious...there is no country in the world where the Christian religion retains a greater influence over the souls of men than in America, and there can be no greater proof of its utility and of its conformity to human nature than that its influence is powerfully felt over the most enlightened and free nation of the earth. In the United States, if a political character attacks a sect [denomination], this may not prevent even the partisans of that very sect from supporting him; but if he attacks all the sects together [Christianity], every one abandons him and he remains alone.

I do not question that the great austerity of manners that is observable in the United States arises, in the first instance, from religious faith.... Its influence over the mind of woman is supreme, and women are the protectors of morals. There is certainly no country in the world where the tie of marriage is more respected than in America or where conjugal happiness is more highly or worthily appreciated.

In the United States the influence of religion is not confined to the manners, but it extends to the intelligence of the people.... Christianity, therefore, reigns without obstacle, by universal consent; the consequence is, as I have before observed, that every principle of the moral world is fixed and determinate.

The safeguard of morality is religion, and morality is the best security of law as well as the surest pledge of freedom.

The Americans combine the notions of Christianity and of liberty so intimately in their minds, that it is impossible to make them conceive the one without the other.

Christianity is the companion of liberty in all its conflicts—the cradle of its infancy, and the divine source of its claims.

They brought with them...a form of Christianity,

which I cannot better describe, than by styling it a democratic and republican religion.... From the earliest settlement of the emigrants, politics and religion contracted an alliance which has never been dissolved.

The Christian nations of our age seem to me to present a most alarming spectacle; the impulse which is bearing them along is so strong that it cannot be stopped, but it is not yet so rapid that it cannot be guided: their fate is in their hands; yet a little while and it may be no longer.[8]

We are rapidly approaching a time of decision. The alarms are resounding, and most assuredly, if we choose to make the divorce final between Lord and liberty, it is only a matter of time before the nation we once knew will, indeed, cease to exist.

Most assuredly the Church has been far from perfect in her own actions throughout the ages. And though certainly not intended, she will likely make more mistakes in the future, as will our federal government. But show me a perfect marriage where neither party makes mistakes. Marriage requires forgiveness, and an unshakable commitment to work through the tough stuff. I for one believe that it is not only possible to return to our former glory, as a nation of Lord and liberty, but that we are also called to surpass this former glory! But it can only happen if we choose to return to our foundations.

Alexis de Tocqueville is also attributed with the following observation, and quite honestly I cannot think of a better way to close this chapter:

I sought for the key to the greatness and genius of America in her harbors...; in her fertile fields and boundless forests; in her rich mines and vast world commerce; in her public school system and institutions of learning. I sought for it in her democratic Congress and in her matchless Constitution.

Not until I went into the churches of America and heard her pulpits flame with righteousness did I understand the secret of her genius and power.

America is great because America is good, and if America ever ceases to be good, America will cease to be great.[9]

Amen!

RECOMMENDED READING

Daniel Dreisback, *Thomas Jefferson and the Wall of Separation Between Church and State*, 2002.

—In-depth, well-researched, and engaging. Speaks to specialist and non-specialist alike. If you want to get a great, balanced perspective on this issue, this is a great place to start!

Notes

1 Encyclopedia-Brittanica, "France, 1715–1789," September 6, 2011. Accessed on January 20, 2012. http://www.britannica.com/EBchecked/topic/215768/France/40384/The-political-response?anchor=ref465174.

2 Ibid.

3 AllAboutHistory.org, "separation of church and state," 2002–2010. Accessed September 26, 2010. http://www.allabouthistory.org/separation-of-church-and-state.htm.

4 Daniel Dreisbach, *Thomas Jefferson and the Wall of Separation Between Church and State* (New York: New York University Press, 2002).

5 Merriam-Webster, "respecting," 2012. Accessed on January 22, 2012. http://www.merriam-webster.com/dictionary/respecting.

6 William J. Federer, *America's God and Country: Encyclopedia of Quotations* (St. Louis: Amerisearch, 2000), 158–161.

7 Merriam-Webster, "religion," 2010. Accessed on September 26, 2010. http://www.merriam-webster.com/dictionary/religion.

8 Federer.

9 Ibid.

~ Fifteen ~

REBUILDING
THE ANCIENT RUINS

As reported earlier in chapter 7, we live in a nation in which 75 to 92 percent of us are professing Christians, according to Gallup between the years of 2008 and 2015.[1] However, a 2005 Gallup poll also reveals that as many as 73 percent of Americans report at least a measure of belief in the paranormal.[2] If this seems inconsistent to some of you, it is; and at the same time, it really is not. You see, not every professing Christian has the same foundation, nor full understanding of what they believe, why they believe it, and what God expects of them. Yet regardless of what we may or may not know, one thing is for certain: People are drawn to the supernatural. And why shouldn't we be? Our Creator is a supernatural God!

Whether you are a professing Christian or not, no person can deny that there is a deep need within each and every one of us to know and touch the supernatural—a desire and a need that comes from our supernatural Creator. Think about it for a moment. If God is supernatural and we are created in His image (as we are told in the book of Genesis), it is only logical that this is also a part of our nature. Yet, instead of embracing and dealing with this aspect of our nature, much of the Church in America has treated supernatural occurrences as the proverbial skeleton in the closet, saying, "Yes, it is there, but do not ask about it. We do not understand it, we cannot control it, and we do not know what to do with it." Hogwash! *Church, if we understood it, it would not be supernatural; and if we could control it, it would not be God!* What we need to know for now is simply this: For everything that is good and real about the supernatural, there is always a counterfeit.

Many people in the Church are even drawn to these counterfeits, including psychics, ESP, Ouija boards, witchcraft, and the like, because they have not been taught that the real thing exists. I cannot tell you how many Christians I have seen with horoscopes posted on their Facebook pages. Why? Because we have stopped expecting God to speak to us, or move supernaturally. We have stopped listening and praying for Him to move because we know that we cannot make Him do it in the way we want or when we want—so in many cases we've stopped trying altogether. Well, guess what? You do not have to seek out the counterfeit anymore. Most people turn to these counterfeits because they want answers—but God Himself can answer you! Need help learning to hear God's voice? Go to church. If your church does not teach you how to hear God's voice, find one that does.

Because the Church of America has been afraid to let the nation see the *supernatural nature* of our Creator working in us and through us, Christians and non-Christians alike have fallen for cheap and unfulfilling substitutes.

There is so much more that we could get into here, but it is not the primary focus of this book. So, for now I encourage you to turn to your local church and trust that God can and *will* use it in your life. Then, once you are moving in the right direction again, plug in, so that you can begin doing the same for others.

For now, I will leave you with the second portion of the word that God gave me for the nation. May it bless you and encourage you. May it inspire you, by the grace of God, to begin rebuilding the age-old foundations of our nation's ruins; may you be called the *"repairer of the breach,"* the *"restorer of the streets"* in which we dwell!

A WORD FROM THE LIVING GOD…PART II

I am not Allah or Buddha…. I am not Baal or any of the million other gods that you have made for yourselves in order to serve your needs. I AM that I AM. And I AM great in mercy, rich in compassion, and slow to anger. I desire nothing more than that you would turn to Me totally and completely, so that I might lavish My love, My favor, and My everlasting blessings upon you.

I have made a way in My Son, Jesus, where there was no way before. He truly is the way, the truth, and the life, and there is no other way but through Him. He holds the keys to the future blessings and success of this country, to her fulfilling her mandate to see freedom established throughout the world—yes, freedom! The mandate of this nation from heaven was not, as some would have you believe, for every American to follow Me or be forced to follow Me, to become a nation of Christians.... I truly do desire that all would come to Me—but not by force. No, her mandate, your mandate as a nation, is that all experience the basic gift I have given in the freedom of choice—whether to accept Me or reject Me—and then to have the freedom to worship Me or not, without penalty of law. I do not judge those who would reject Me while they yet live—for what I have said is true: I desire mercy and not judgment. Rarely do I serve up judgment while any yet live, but rather I choose to show mercy and love in the hope that all will come to know Me through My Son and through His Bride (the Church), that they would come to repentance and receive the gift of eternal life.

I desire that, through the basic freedoms that have been established in the United States, people would then be able to discover the true freedom that I have to offer, which has often been portrayed as bondage, even by those who would follow Me. True freedom is My desire for all men and women of all nations. But for many, before this can happen they need to taste of the basic freedom that I have given to you to model as a nation. The mandate has been given to many countries throughout the ages. But as each has turned from Me and thus left the mandate, I have thence passed the torch on to another, and another, and another, until at last it has been passed to you. It was not King George III who incited your ancestors to revolution, but rather it was I who chose you and established you, because Britain had relinquished the very mandate that you now carry. "One nation, under God, indivisible," was My idea!

Read your own history books. Your country was not birthed by chance, luck, or mere good fortune any more than the earth was created by some fictional, evolutionary "big bang"! I created the heavens and the earth and created man in Our own image...and it was I, just the same, who established this great nation in which you now enjoy these basic freedoms and inalienable rights that so many take for granted and that some have secretly devised to undermine. But their plans will not prevail, for I am calling forth the spirit of revolution once more to awaken this nation, that she might shine far brighter than ever before. A revolution not fought or won by the force of arms this time, but by the use of still greater weapons...prayer, truth, and love!

Kings, queens, prime ministers, presidents, and the like can all be established or removed through the power of prayer. And no one takes authority whom I have not allowed to have it. My truth spoken in the heart of love, with My timing, can disarm and dismantle an enemy quicker than any band of special forces in any branch of your loyal, honorable, and prestigious military.

Truly the glory of the latter house shall be greater than the glory of the former! **I am not looking to bring you back to what you once were...but I am calling you forth to become what you have been called and commissioned to be as a nation...a steward and a defender of freedoms.** A good steward is never content to merely keep what he has been entrusted with by his master, but rather he desires to seek growth of the very thing that he stewards. As a nation, I charge you and encourage you once again to defend and to steward the freedoms that I have established by My grace, and in My strength…for only under Me shall you remain "one nation…indivisible, with liberty and justice for all."

RECOMMENDED READING

Bill Johnson, *When Heaven Invades Earth*, 2003.

—Sound, biblical, and practical. Johnson does an excellent job in helping us to reconnect to the supernatural God of the Bible and learn what it takes to experience Him firsthand. An easy read, whether you are familiar with Christianity or not.

Notes

1 Frank Newport, "Easter Season Finds a Religious, Largely Christian, Nation," *Gallup*, March 21, 2008. Accessed on June 11, 2010. Frank Newport, "This Christmas, 78% of Americans Identify as Christian," *Gallup*, December 24, 2009. Accessed on January 7, 2012. http://www.gallup.com/poll/124793/This-Christmas-78-Americans-Identify-Christian.aspx; Frank Newport, "Percentage of Christians in U.S. Drifting Down, but Still High," *Gallup*, December 24, 2015. Accessed on February 28, 2016. http://www.gallup.com/poll/187955/percentage-christians-drifting-down-high.aspx.

2 David W. Moore, "Wellbeing: Three in Four Americans Believe in Paranormal," *Gallup*, June 16, 2005. Accessed on September 26, 2010. http://www.gallup.com/poll/16915/Three-Four-Americans-Believe-Paranormal.aspx.

~ Sixteen ~

STAND, PRAY, ACT

Above all I must avoid politics…—John Adams

Even the most committed man of principle will struggle with the thought of acting upon conviction if it means risking everything. John Adams was no different. After his brilliant performance in defending the British soldiers accused in the Boston Massacre, his rise to fame was inevitable. He stood on his convictions at a time when no one else dared to do so, and he earned for himself the reputation of being an honorable man. As an attorney, he traveled a circuit of more than two hundred miles from the island of Martha's Vineyard, north to Maine, and as far west as Worcester, handling every type of case. "He saw every side of life, learned to see things as they were, and was considered, as Jonathan Sewall would write, as 'honest [a] lawyer as ever broke bread.'"[1]

Indeed, Adams had quickly become Boston's busiest attorney, and he was doing quite well for himself. Some might say that he was at the peak of his career, gaining wealth, buying land, and prospering greatly. He was even offered the position of "advocate general in the Court of Admiralty" at the request of the governor of Massachusetts. It was a position of not only great honor and prestige, but one that would open the door to some of the most profitable business in the province. Nevertheless, it was also a position that he would refuse to take—due to his convictions and differences with the British Crown.[2]

In fact, despite his newfound wealth and popularity, Adams continued to grow more and more restless. He had seen firsthand the injustices being perpetrated by King George III upon the people of the American colonies, and he filled the pages of his journal with his thoughts about government and freedom. However:

> At the same time, he was vowing, at least in the privacy of his diary, to devote himself wholly to his private business and providing for his family. "Above all things I must avoid politics..." But as tensions in the colony mounted, so did his pent-up rage and longing for action.[3]

It appears that things finally came to a head for Mr. Adams while he was socializing with some friends one evening. In the midst of their time together, a visiting Englishman began praising the English sense of justice. Adams exploded, surprising everyone—including himself— by exclaiming that "there is no more justice in Britain than in hell!" Having so clearly revealed his heart, he at last relented and set himself upon a course that would soon find him chosen as one of five delegates to the first Continental Congress at Philadelphia in 1774—a course that would ultimately see him pledge, "with a firm reliance on the protection of Divine Providence," his life, his fortune, and his sacred honor, for the establishment of a new nation.[4] To be certain, President Adams, as well as many others, sacrificed much to stand upon their convictions.

CLARITY OF CONVICTION

Conviction is essentially this—a strong and firmly held belief. It is quite likely that you held a few convictions of your own before ever picking up this book. Perhaps this book has challenged you to refine or redefine some convictions that you have held all of your life. Other readers, however, might be realizing for the first time that they have never really held any strong convictions. Does it matter? Can life be lived without any convictions? Yes it can, but the truth is this—a life without conviction will always lack fulfillment. Without firmly held beliefs, you will always be at the mercy of others as they lead you here and there based on their own convictions, for better or for worse.

However, when we hold, challenge, and cultivate our own convictions, they can then guide us, direct us, and ultimately help us find purpose in our lives. Most importantly, we need to explore our convictions with regard to the God of the universe and His desire to speak and interact with us. The convictions of John Adams and our Founding Fathers—of God's existence, His love for us, and His desire to interact with us—have long directed this nation with purpose. It has been our consolation and source of hope in times of sorrow, such as after the terrorist attacks of September 11, 2001.

By themselves, convictions that are not acted upon lead to nothing more than frustration, dissatisfaction, and bitterness. Don't believe me? Listen to any frustrated, dissatisfied, bitter person whom you know. In doing so, you will often find that they are constantly complaining about things that are going on in their city, church, school system, the government, their workplace—things that they have likely never acted upon or followed through on, in an attempt to make a bad situation better. They are typically full of good intentions and ideas, but they lack the courage to act. *Conviction requires action for fulfillment!*

COURAGE TO ACT

Because conviction is a belief, it therefore necessitates faith, and faith is spelled *R-I-S-K*. Regardless of how many facts we may have collected on an issue, they are worthless unless we are willing to take a chance by standing in faith upon the convictions to which those facts have led us. Acting upon our convictions is risky business. Our forefathers and many others throughout the history of this great nation have risked everything in order to act upon the conviction that "all men were created equal." They risked everything, including their very lives, to see this conviction brought to fulfillment.

For example, when our Constitution was framed, the intent was laid out that slavery needed to be abolished in this new nation. While our Founders predominantly held the conviction that slavery was an abomination to both God and humanity, they chose not to act upon that conviction to its fullest extent. In other words, right or wrong, they did not make a push to end slavery immediately, due to their fear of seeing the Union dissolve before it was ever fully established. However, they did make the provision that while slavery would be preserved for the first twenty years of our nation's history, after that point it would no longer be a protected institution. This was done in the hopes that the volatile nature of the issue would die down enough in two decades' time to allow it to be addressed in such a manner that *all* men could finally be said to be free and equal—black or white, slave or free. Even the ex-slave Frederick Douglass would later say of the Constitution:

> Now, take the [C]onstitution according to its plain reading, and I defy the presentation of a single proslavery clause in it. On the other hand, it will be found to contain principles and purposes, entirely hostile to the existence of slavery.[5]

The intention was clearly there. Yet, in spite of that, the year 1807 came and went, and slavery still remained. Therefore, it became necessary for others to pick up the torch to see freedom more fully established, as was the true intent of our founding documents. That notwithstanding, the Constitution of this nation remains an excellent example of the convictions of our Founding Fathers, which were acted upon to the best of their abilities.

CONSTITUTIONAL CRISIS

In recent years, many of our politicians have sought to bypass, disregard, or utterly ignore the Constitution of this nation, a document that each of them promises to uphold when they are sworn into office. According to many of them, it is nothing more than a "living document," which to them means that it needs to "change with the people and the times." However, instead of seeking to actually make changes to the Constitution, something that can and has been done many times, they use this terminology to do whatever they wish, counting on the ignorance of the American people to allow it. If they truly held their convictions, they would be seeking to change things openly and legally, but they do not.

Our Constitution, in its original form, is not infallible. Yet before we begin making all sorts of changes to reflect the so-called enlightenment of the day and age in which we now live, we need to carefully and critically examine what was intended by this document, which took years to find a consensus of conviction upon, and over which much blood was spilled for its establishment and protection. If we presently stand unaware of the issues of questionable legality with regard to our Constitution today, we need to make ourselves aware. It is time to begin doing our own homework by critically looking at both sides of an issue instead of relying upon others to do this for us. We can no longer afford to vote based upon the opinions and convictions of others at this point in our nation's history—too much is at stake.

FOUNDATIONAL NATURE OF PRAYER

Much could be said to firmly establish the notion that our Founders did, in fact, pray in their personal lives, as well as in the public and political arenas. Read *America's God and Country* by Federer, or any of the other hundreds of historical books and documents that are available to you—read them for yourself. We are undeniably a nation of prayer. Our Founders did not rely upon God because of religion; they did so because time and again, He had acted on their behalf to provide, preserve, and even defend them and this nation in miraculous ways. According to George Washington, it was "by the miraculous care of Providence" that he escaped unharmed in the battle near the Monongahela in 1755.[6] Writing to his brother about this, Washington stated that by the end of

185

that battle, he had found four bullet holes in his coat and had two horses shot out from under him. Legend even tells of an Indian chief who met Washington some fifteen years later and spoke to him of that day, saying that he had "seventeen fair fires" at Washington with his rifle, but he still could not bring him down.[7] Time and again God has provided for America, whether we have seen it, read about it, heard about it, or not.

SOVEREIGNTY VERSUS CONTROL

Contrary to popular belief, God is *not* in control. This idea is nowhere to be found in God's Word. However, what *is* true is that God is *sovereign* and He loves to interact with, and on behalf of, all of His creation. The truth is that *we* are in control through our choices and our actions, while also being impacted by the choices and actions of others. The messes that we find ourselves in, for which we often choose to blame God, are frequently a result of choices we or others make. He can intervene whenever and wherever He wants or desires to, but He chooses not to interfere with our free will. I don't know why God chooses to act in some situations and not in others, but I do know this:

He is dependable whether I see Him act or not. He is dependable whether He acts in the way that I think He should or not.

Think of it this way: As parents, friends, or coworkers, we sometimes choose to intervene in the lives of our children, friends, or coworkers, and sometimes we do not. Why? Because sometimes it is in their best interest for us to do so, and other times it is not. We can see from our perspective why we choose to or not, yet they may not be able to understand this perspective. Does that then make us uncaring or less dependable, because they cannot see things from our point of view? No! It's merely an obstacle that needs to be overcome in our relationship, but it can be resolved through good communication and by getting to know each other better. In the same way, I know God is dependable because I have a relationship with Him. I know Him, and He reveals Himself to me in the same way He desires to reveal Himself to you and to all of humanity. *Prayer is not foundational because it is traditional; it is traditionally foundational because God is dependable!*

CLOSING THOUGHTS...

In doing my own research and reading over the past several years while I have been writing this book, I ran across this statement:

Securing a revolution has proven to be a much more daunting assignment than winning one.[8]

If this is true, and we acknowledge that our reliance upon God was vitally necessary in the establishment of this great nation, then we must now all the more choose to rely upon Him as we seek to secure the freedoms and liberties that were fought and paid for by those who went before us. To be certain, there will be a cost in every generation if freedom is to be defended and preserved. But this does not just happen by electing the "right" people. It is a process of conviction and submission.

Submission is nothing more than getting under, and then pushing up to support the mission of another. First and foremost, I implore you to submit yourselves to the living God, and here we need to begin with individuals. Establish a relationship, learn to hear His voice, and seek firsthand revelation from Him. It is good to have books like this, through which He can speak, but this is never meant to be your main source of hearing from God. Even the Bible, which is meant to be one of our main sources of communication from God, requires interaction with Him as we read it. You do not need to wait for the next book to be published, or for your pastor or priest to speak. God promises that those who will seek Him will indeed find Him and they will not be disappointed. In the process, we need to begin refining our convictions with His help, and then determine to act upon those convictions at His leading, regardless of the cost.

Second, we need to submit ourselves to our families, to support the family mission by teaching our children and helping them form and embrace convictions, as well. For far too long parents have relinquished the responsibility to raise their children, and instead they have relied upon others to do so through public or even private schools, after-school programs, day care, and the like. It is okay to utilize these resources, but we should never allow them to become the primary source to instill moral character and virtue in our children. If we do not choose to invest ourselves in our children, we will most assuredly create more problems than we solve. We may set ourselves upon the task of protecting freedom and fighting injustice, but at the same time we will be releasing a generation who will trample the very things we are seeking to establish. The family unit is under assault in this nation—it is time to actively pursue the restoration of the family and begin by fighting back, one family at a time.

Finally, submit yourselves to one another. We have allowed our government and the mainstream media to set wedges between us based upon our financial status, our race, past offenses, and more. But it is time to look beyond those differences. It is time to carefully listen to one another, forgive, and discover that we have much more in common than what we have been led to believe. And, if this is true, then it is time for us to stand, as a nation of patriotic and compassionate individuals, on the common ground established by the living God for the preservation of our beloved free nation.

Now is the time to stand on conviction and pray, and to be convicted by that prayer to act. For neither prayer nor action will ever be enough by themselves.

RECOMMENDED READING

William J. Federer, *America's God and Country, Encyclopedia of Quotations*, 2000.
—Great book on numerous topics with quotes, excerpts, and references from diaries, congressional records, speeches, and more from many of America's historical figures.

Notes

1 David McCullough, *John Adams* (New York: Simon and Schuster, 2001), 63–65, 69–70.

2 Ibid.

3 Ibid.

4 Ibid.

5 William J. Bennett, *America: The Last Best Hope*, Volume 1 (Nashville: Thomas Nelson, 2006), 125.

6 Michael and Jana Novak, *Washington's God* (New York: Basic Books, 2006), 56.

7 Ibid.

8 Joseph J. Ellis, *Founding Brothers: The Revolutionary Generation* (New York: Vintage, 2000), 78.

APPENDIX

If you are in need of personal assistance in this process of transforming your life, from being a victim to living in victory, or in dealing with any of the subject matter that has been brought forth in the first half of this book, here are a few other suggestions of resources you might check into:

Your local Christian church: Pray about it, and then ask God to direct you to a local church within your community that will best serve your needs. When you're done praying, trust that He'll guide you to the right place, and also that He is able to make it quite clear if you are in the wrong place.

Elijah House Ministries http://www.elijahhouse.org/: If you believe you are in need of more in-depth counseling, here is a great place to start.

About the Author

FRED GARCIA lives in Genoa, Ohio, with his wife, Michele, and their three children. A graduate of Bowling Green State University, Fred has been a practicing physical therapist for the past twenty-two years. Fred is also a graduate of "RAIN" Bible School and an ordained minister. He is the Senior Pastor of Christ Community Church in Genoa, where he and his family have served in various aspects of ministry over the past seventeen years. He is an accomplished musician, songwriter, author, teacher, and caring family man. He has served across the denominations throughout his years of ministry and greatly appreciates the beauty and diversity of the body of Christ.

Contact Information
To inquire about having Fred and his family share with your group, please contact him at:

Email: fredgarcia1971@gmail.com

on Facebook:

https://www.facebook.com/Fred-Garcia-153798697999926/

website: http://www.restorersawake.com